2nd Workshop on Semantics-Driven Statistical Machine Translation (SedMT 2016)

Held at the 2016 Conference of the North American Chapter of the Association for Computational Linguistics: Human Language Technologies (NAACL HLT 2016)

San Diego, California, USA
16 June 2016

ISBN: 978-1-5108-2524-6

Printed from e-media with permission by:

Curran Associates, Inc.
57 Morehouse Lane
Red Hook, NY 12571

Some format issues inherent in the e-media version may also appear in this print version.

Printed by Curran Associates, Inc. (2016)

For permission requests, please contact the Association for Computational Linguistics at the address below.

Association for Computational Linguistics
209 N. Eighth Street
Stroudsburg, Pennsylvania 18360

Phone: 1-570-476-8006
Fax: 1-570-476-0860

acl@aclweb.org

Additional copies of this publication are available from:

Curran Associates, Inc.
57 Morehouse Lane
Red Hook, NY 12571 USA
Phone: 845-758-0400
Fax: 845-758-2634
Email: curran@proceedings.com
Web: www.proceedings.com

Proceedings of the 2nd Workshop on Semantics-Driven Machine Translation (SedMT 2016)

The 2nd Workshop on Semantics-Driven Machine Translation

Deyi Xiong, Kevin Duh, Eneko Agirre,
Nora Aranberri and Houfeng Wang (editors)

June 16, 2016
San Diego, California, USA

Preface

We are very pleased to welcome you to the 2nd Workshop on Semantics-Driven Machine Translation (SedMT) in conjunction with NAACL, held on June 16, 2016 in San Diego, California, USA.

It is widely recognized that machine translation inherently requires semantics to obtain meaning representations of source sentences and to generate meaning-preserving target translations. Recent years have witnessed a resurgent huge interest in exploring semantics for machine translation, e.g., employing lexical semantics for word sense and semantic role disambiguation in machine translation, using compositional semantics for phrasal translation, incorporating discourse semantics into document-level machine translation and so on. The emerging neural machine translation (NMT) is also naturally born as semantic machine translation since it heavily relies on distributional semantic representations.

This workshop seeks to build on the success of its precursor S2MT 2015 (http://hlt.suda.edu.cn/workshop/s2mt/index.html), which was held in conjunction with ACL 2015 in Beijing. S2MT 2015 brought together a large number of researchers from the machine translation and semantics community. Its program included high-quality papers examining and exploring semantics in machine translation from different angles and perspectives. It also featured 4 keynote speeches covering topics that cross boundaries of semantics and machine translation, as well as a thought-provoking panel discussion on the gaps and challenges between semantics and statistical machine translation.

This workshop will continue efforts of promoting the shift of interest from syntax to semantics in machine translation, exploring new horizons and cultivating ideas of cutting-edge models and algorithms for semantic machine translation.

After a rigorous selection, we only accepted 2 high-quality papers to be presented in the workshop program. These two papers study language constructions from a semantic perspective. In particular, Alastair Butler investigates the generation of several typical language constructions of English for machine translation with meaning representation informed decisions. Shili Ge and Rou Song discover 5 different construction patterns for clauses in Chinese-English translation.

In addition to the accepted papers, we also accepted two extended abstracts. Extended abstracts are 2-3 pages long. Since this is the first time to include extended abstracts in the workshop program, we invite contributions from team members of semantic MT projects and semantic MT researchers worldwide. Liangyou Li, Andy Way and Qun Liu incorporate dependency semantics into graph-based machine translation. Kiril Simov, Petya Osenova and Alex Popov examine hybrid MT system with word sense annotations on the source side for Bulgarian-English Translation.

Following the tradition of the former workshop, we invited 4 distinguished keynote speakers from semantics and machine translation to cover topics that cross boundaries of these two areas. Johan Bos (University of Groningen) will give a talk on building a large parallel meaning bank for four languages, i.e., English, Dutch, German and Italian. Jan Hajic (Charles University in Prague) will give a speech on the Chimera-TectoMT architecture of machine translation with deep linguistic analysis. Kyunghyun Cho (New York University) will give a talk on the latest research on neural machine translation without explicit linguistic structures. Martha Palmer (University of Colorado) will give a talk on designing abstract meaning representations for machine translation. The former two keynote speeches will be in the morning session while the later two talks in the afternoon session.

The workshop will organize a panel discussion on "What semantic phenomena/annotations/forms are most promising for traditional SMT or NMT?" at the end of the program.

We would like to thank the whole Program Committee, the invited keynote and panel speakers and all authors who submitted papers to the workshop. We acknowledge the general support from our sponsors QTLeap project and the National Science Foundation of China and Jiangsu Province (grants No. 61403269 and BK20140355).

Organizers of the SedMT workshop
Deyi Xiong, Kevin Duh, Eneko Agirre, Nora Aranberri and Houfeng Wang

Organizers:

Deyi Xiong, Soochow University
Kevin Duh, Johns Hopkins University Human Language Technology Center of Excellence
Eneko Agirre, University of the Basque Country
Nora Aranberri, University of the Basque Country
Houfeng Wang, Peking University

Program Committee:

Rafael E. Banchs, Institute for Infocomm Research
Johan Bos, University of Groningen
Boxing Chen, National Research Council Canada
David Chiang, University of Notre Dame
Michael Goodman, Nanyang Technological University
Jan Hajic, Charles University in Prague
Zhongjun He, Baidu
Shujian Huang, Nanjing University
Kevin Knight, ISI
Philipp Koehn, Johns Hopkins University
Qun Liu, Dublin City University
Yang Liu, Tsinghua University
Chi-kiu Lo, National Research Council Canada
Wei Lu, Singapore University of Technology and Design
Zhengdong Lu, Noahs Ark Lab, Huawei Technologies
Minh-Thang Luong, Stanford University
Preslav Nakov, Qatar Computing Research Institute
Hwee-Tou Ng, National University of Singapore
Martha Palmer, University of Colorado
Lane Schwartz, University of Illinois
Khalil Sima'an, University of Amsterdam
Jinsong Su, Xiamen University
Hans Uszkoreit, Saarland University
Tong Xiao , Northeastern University
Frances Yung, Nara Institute of Science and Technology
Dongdong Zhang, Microsoft Research Asia
Jiajun Zhang, Institute of Automation, Chinese Academy of Sciences
Yue Zhang, Singapore University of Technology and Design

Invited Speakers:

Johan Bos, University of Groningen
Kyunghyun Cho, New York University
Jan Hajic, Charles University in Prague
Martha Palmer, University of Colorado

Panelists:

Johan Bos, University of Groningen
Kyunghyun Cho, New York University
Jan Hajic, Charles University in Prague
Martha Palmer, University of Colorado

Sponsors:

QTLeap
National Science Foundation of China (grant No. 61403269)
National Science Foundation of Jiangsu Province (grant No. BK20140355)

Proceedings Editor:

Xing Wang, Soochow University

Keynote Speech (I)
Building a Large Parallel Meaning Bank

Johan Bos
University of Groningen
johan.bos@rug.nl

Abstract

Translating from one language into another is a complex task and *meaning*, undoubtly, plays a crucial role (Langeveld, 1986). As anyone knows, there are good and bad translations. A good, faithful translation implies that all nuances of meaning have been preserved in the process of translating from one language to another. Bad translations show unwanted changes in meaning, and are often obtained by "blind" word-by-word substitutions, known to be not necessarily meaning preserving. For instance, literally translating "having a chat" into the Dutch phrase "een praatje hebben" changes the meaning and is therefore considered a bad translation. Paradoxically, often slight differences in meaning *are* allowed in translations: "voetballer" could be translated as "player" in football contexts.

As a matter of fact, meaning-preserving translations are not always possible, because there are 'lexical gaps' between languages, often caused by cultural differences. For example, in English there is a distinction between *cousin* and *nephew*, in Dutch it is just *neef.* There is no single Dutch word for *siblings*, one would say *broers en zussen.* Italian *sentire* generalizes over both the English *to hear*, *to feel* and *to taste.* Many national dishes or habits cannot be translated directly into other languages (e.g. Dutch *stroopwafel* is hard to catch in one Italian word; Italian *buonasera* needs to be translated as *good afternoon* when expressed at 2pm, but as *good evening* when used at 7pm). Some colour terms have no one-to-one correspondence between languages, e.g. *blue*: in Italian *blu* (dark blue), *azzurro* (light blue), or *celeste* (paler blue).

To investigate these phenomena from a semantic perspective on a massive scale one needs (a) a substantial number of translations, (b) meaning representations of these translations, and (c) being able to recognize non-literal interpretations. For a long time, since the interest in research of automated translation, this was simply not possible. But nowadays large parallel corpora exist and (very recently) substantial progress has been made in automated semantic interpretation. The aim of this project is to find out what the conditions are that determine good or bad translations, and investigate what role meaning plays in this process. The key idea is to automatically analyze large collections of translated texts (a technique that drastically improved current machine translation systems in the last decade) and assign cross-lingual formal meaning representations to the translations (Evang and Bos, 2013; Bos, 2014). We hope that this computational approach will offer us a completely new view on the relationship between meaning and translation by building a parallel meaning bank for four languages (English, Dutch, German and Italian). It could also be used to improve machine translation by developing translation quality metrics based on meaning rather than plain words.

Biography

Johan Bos is Professor of Computational Semantics at the University of Groningen. He received his doctorate from the Computational Linguistics Department at the University of the Saarland in 2001. Since then, he held post-doc positions at the University of Edinburgh, working on spoken dialogue systems, and the La Sapienza University of Rome, conducting research on automated question answering. In 2010 he moved to his current position in Groningen, leading the computational semantics group. Bos is the developer of Boxer, a state-of-the-art wide-coverage semantic parser for English, nitiator of the Groningen Meaning Bank, a large semantically-annotated corpus of texts, and inventor of Wordrobe, a game with a purpose for semantic annotation. Bos is PI of an NWO VICI-project "Lost in Translation – Found in Meaning" investigating the role of meaning in human and machine translation. He is also current president of the ACL special interest group in computational semantics (SIGSEM).

References

Johan Bos. 2014. Semantic annotation issues in parallel meaning banking. In Proceedings of the Tenth Joint ACL-ISO Workshop on Interoperable Semantic Annotation (ISA-10), pages 17–20, Reykjavik, Iceland.

Kilian Evang and Johan Bos. 2013. Using parallel corpora to bootstrap multilingual semantic parsers. In 20 Years of Bitext workshop at EMNLP 2013, Seattle, WA, USA.

Arthur Langeveld. 1986. Vertalen wat er staat. Synthese, De arbeiderspers.

Keynote Speech (II)
The Chimera-TectoMT architecture of Machine Translation with Deep Linguistic Analysis

Jan Hajic
Charles University in Prague
hajic@ufal.mff.cuni.cz

Abstract

The TectoMT system is a result of long-term development which began in the pre-statistical era at Charles University in Prague and continued to include state-of-the-art tools for POS tagging, morphological feature disambiguation, lemmatization parsing, and some aspects of semantic analysis. It follows the usual Analysis-Transfer-Generation workflow, with transfer trained on a large parallel corpus using Hidden Markov Tree Model. Generation is partly rule-based (at the syntax level) and partly statistical (at the inflection/morphology level). Chimera is a hybrid system that uses a specific combination of TectoMT and a standard Phrase-based SMT (Moses), complemented by a "Depfix" automatic post-editing system, which as a whole improves on the individual systems, as documented in the results of the recent WMT Shared tasks. The system has been originally developed for English-Czech and recently transferred to several other languages within the EU QTLeap project (qtleap.eu), where it has been successfully used in the IT domain for both question and answer translation in a Q&A context. Both the TectoMT and Chimera systems will be presented together with a discussion about language (in) dependence of such a hybrid solution.

Biography

Jan Hajic is a full professor of Computational Linguistics at the Institute of Formal and Applied Linguistics, School of Computer Science (Faculty of Mathematics and Physics) at the Charles University in Prague, Czech Republic and has an Adjunct professor appointment at the Computer Science Department at the University of Colorado in Boulder. His interests cover morphology of inflective languages, machine translation, deep language understanding, and the application of statistical methods in natural language processing in general. He has also built a number of richly annotated language resources. His work experience includes both industrial research (IBM Research, Yorktown Heights, 1991-1993) and academia (Charles University, Prague and Johns Hopkins University, Baltimore, MD, USA). He has been the PI or Co-PI of several national and international grants and projects, most notably the large Czech Grant Agency grant for the Center of Computational Linguistics (2005-2011), several EU projects on Machine Translation (EuroMatrix/Plus, Faust, QTLeap, META-NET; currently HimL, QT21 and CRACKER) and the U.S.-based large ITR project "Malach" (coordinated by the Visual History Foundation, Los Angeles, CA, USA). Currently he is head of the large national infrastructure project "LINDAT/CLARIN" (2010-2019) and a deputy director of the Institute; he is the Chairman of the Board of META-NET, European network for multilingual language technology. He has about 110 cited publications, including a book on computational inflectional morphology.

Keynote Speech (III)

Statistical Machine Translation *without* Explicit Linguistic Structures

Kyunghyun Cho
Computer Science and Data Science,
New York University
kyunghyun.cho@nyu.edu

Abstract

Different linguistic structures exist at various levels of natural language. A word is composed of a lexeme and a number of morphemes. A phrase consists of multiple words. Multiple phrases form a sentence. A paragraph is a sequence of more than one sentences, and so on. These structures, be them syntactic or semantic, facilitate our analysis of natural languages. It is however unclear whether these structures are necessary for machine translation. In this talk, I will present some of the latest research in neural machine translation, where nearly no such linguistic structure is being exploited, however, with comparable to, or often better than, many existing machine translation systems. The goal of this talk is not to strongly assert that those linguistic structures are not necessary, but to stimulate active discussion on this issue.

Biography

Kyunghyun Cho is an assistant professor of Computer Science and Data Science at New York University (NYU). Previously, he was a postdoctoral researcher at the University of Montreal under the supervision of Prof. Yoshua Bengio after obtaining a doctorate degree at Aalto University (Finland) in early 2014. Kyunghyun's main research interests include neural networks, generative models and their applications.

Keynote Speech (IV)
Designing Abstract Meaning Representations

Martha Palmer
Departments of Computer Science and Linguistics
University of Colorado
Martha.Palmer@colorado.edu

Abstract

Abstract Meaning Representations (AMRs) provide a single, graph-based semantic representation that abstracts away from the word order and syntactic structure of a sentence, resulting in a more language-neutral representation of its meaning. Current versions of AMRs capture nested predicate argument structures with PropBank-style semantic role labels, Named Entity tags, coreference, discourse relations and explicit interpretations of modality and negation. AMRs implement a simplified, standard neo-Davidsonian semantics. A word in a sentence either maps to a concept or a relation or is omitted if it is already inherent in the representation or it conveys inter-personal attitude (e.g., stance or distancing), (Banarescu et al., 2013). The basis of AMR is the PropBank lexicon of coarse-grained senses of verb, noun and adjective relations as well as the roles associated with each sense (each lexicon entry is a 'roleset') (Palmer et al., 2005). By marking the appropriate roles for each sense, this level of annotation provides information regarding *who* is doing *what* to *whom*. However, unlike PropBank, AMR provides a deeper level of representation of discourse relations, non-relational noun and prepositional phrases, quantities and time expressions (which PropBank largely leaves unanalyzed). Additionally, AMR makes a greater effort to abstract away from language-particular syntactic facts, instead attempting to generalize what can be thought of as different ways of saying the same thing. This talk will explore the differences between PropBank and AMR, the current and future plans for AMR annotation, and the potential of AMR as a basis for machine translation (Xue et al., 2014).

Biography

Martha Palmer is a Professor at the University of Colorado with joint appointments in Linguistics and Computer Science, an Institute of Cognitive Science Faculty Fellow, and the Director of CLEAR, the Computational Language and EducAtion Research Center. She also directed the 2011 Linguistics Institute in Boulder. Professor Palmer's Ph.D. is in Artificial Intelligence from the University of Edinburgh, in 1985. She is an Association of Computational Linguistics (ACL) Fellow, and has won an Outstanding Graduate Advisor 2014 Award and a Boulder Faculty Assembly 2010 Research Award. Her research is focused on capturing elements of the meanings of words that can comprise automatic representations of complex sentences and documents. Supervised machine learning techniques rely on vast amounts of annotated training data so she and her students are engaged in providing data with semantic annotation for English, Chinese, Arabic, Hindi, and Urdu, funded by DARPA and NSF, both manually and automatically. A more recent focus is the application of these methods to biomedical journal articles and clinical notes, funded by NIH, and also to the Geosciences (ClearEarth), funded by NSF. She co-edits LiLT, Linguistic Issues in Language Technology, and has been a co-editor of the Journal of Natural Language Engineering and on the CLJ Editorial Board. She is a past President of ACL, and past Chair of SIGLEX and of SIGHAN.

Acknowledgments

The content of this talk represents the fruit of a large, long-term collaborative effort that has involved valuable input from all of the co-authors of the papers cited, but which has especially benefited from the thoughts and guidance of Kevin Knight, Daniel Marcu, Ulf Hermjakob, Claire Bonial, Tim O'Gorman, Kira Griffit, Nathan Schneider, Nianwen Xue, Jan Hajic and Zdenka Uresova. We also gratefully acknowledge the support of the National Science Foundation CISE-IISRI-0910992, Richer Representations for Machine Translation, and DARPA DEFT - FA-8750-13-2-0045 (a subcontract from LDC). Any opinions, findings, and conclusions or recommendations expressed in this material are those of the authors and do not necessarily reflect the views of the National Science Foundation.

References

Laura Banarescu, Claire Bonial, Shu Cai, Madalina Georgescu, Kira Griffitt, Ulf Hermjakob, Kevin Knight, Philipp Koehn, Martha Palmer, and Nathan Schneider. 2013. Abstract meaning representation for sembanking. In Proceedings of the 7th Linguistic Annotation Workshop and Interoperability with Discourse, pages 178–186. Association for Computational Linguistics.

Martha Palmer, Daniel Gildea, and Paul Kingsbury. 2005. The Proposition Bank: An annotated corpus of semantic roles. Computational Linguistics, 31(1):71–106.

Nianwen Xue, Ondrej Bojar, Jan Hajic, Martha Palmer, Zdenka Uresova, and Xiuhong Zhang. 2014. Not an interlingua, but close: Comparison of english amrs to chinese and czech. In Proceedings of the Sixth International Conference on Language Resources and Evaluation(LREC).

Table of Contents

Workshop Program

Thursday, June 16, 2016

8:45–9:00 ***Opening Remarks***

9:00–10:30 **Session 1 (Chair: Yvette Graham)**

9:00–10:00 *Keynote Speech (I)*
Building a Large Parallel Meaning Bank
Johan Bos (University of Groningen)

10:00–10:15 *Deterministic natural language generation from meaning representations for machine translation*
Alastair Butler

10:15–10:30 *Extending Phrase-Based Translation with Dependencies by Using Graphs*
Liangyou Li, Andy Way and Qun Liu

10:30–11:00 ***Coffee Break***

11:00–12:00 **Session 2 (Chair: Nora Aranberri)**

11:00–12:00 *Keynote Speech (II)*
The Chimera-TectoMT architecture of Machine Translation with Deep Linguistic Analysis
Jan Hajic (Charles University in Prague)

12:00–14:00 ***Lunch***

Thursday, June 16, 2016 (continued)

14:00–15:30 Session 3 (Chair: Andrew Finch)

14:00–15:00 *Keynote Speech (III)*
Statistical Machine Translation without Explicit Linguistic Structures
Kyunghyun Cho (New York University)

15:00–15:15 *The Naming Sharing Structure and its Cognitive Meaning in Chinese and English*
Shili Ge and Rou Song

15:15–15:30 *Towards Semantic-based Hybrid Machine Translation between Bulgarian and English*
Kiril Simov, Petya Osenova and Alexander Popov

15:30–16:00 *Coffee Break*

16:00–17:45 Session 4 (Chair: Nora Aranberri)

16:00–17:00 *Keynote Speech (IV)*
Designing Abstract Meaning Representations
Martha Palmer (University of Colorado)

17:00–17:45 *Panel*
What semantic phenomena/annotations/forms are most promising for traditional SMT or NMT?
Panelists: Johan Bos, Kyunghyun Cho, Jan Hajic, Martha Palmer

17:45 *Closing*

Deterministic natural language generation from meaning representations for machine translation

Alastair Butler
National Institute for Japanese Language and Linguistics
ajb129@hotmail.com

Abstract

This paper describes a deterministic method for generating natural language suited to being part of a machine translation system with meaning representations as the level for language transfer. Starting from Davidsonian/Penman meaning representations, syntactic trees are built following the Penn Parsed Corpus of Modern British English, from which the yield (i.e., the words) can be taken. The novel contribution is to highlight exploiting the presentation of meaning content to inform decisions regarding the selection of language constructions: active vs. passive, argument subject vs. expletive it vs. existential there, discourse vs. intra-sentential coordination vs. adverbial clause vs. participial clause vs. purpose clause, and infinitive clause vs. finite clause vs. small clause vs. relative clause vs. it cleft.

1 Introduction

This paper pursues the idea that the arrangement of information contained by a meaning representation can provide sufficient clues to drive a deterministic generation of natural language. This is particularly suited to being part of a machine translation system with meaning representations as the level for language transfer because the clues exploited for generating the target language can be gathered when converting the source language to a meaning representation. The paper is structured as follows. Section 2 gives background for the approach. Section 3 sketches the generation procedure with a simple example. Section 4 is the core of the paper, detailing different grammatical constructions and triggers for their creation. Section 5 is a conclusion.

2 Background

The generation of this paper aims to form part of a pipeline approach to machine translation, where a semantic parser transforms source language sentences into meaning representations that are inputs for generation to produce target language sentences.

While many semantic parsing systems are now available, representations reached are typically either (neo-)Davidsonian predicate language formulas (Davidson, 1967; Parsons, 1990; Landman 2000), or Penman style representations (Matthiessen and Bateman, 1991). Generation in this paper will start from Penman representations that are derived from Davidsonian predicate language formulas. Systems producing (neo-)Davidsonian output are typically based on methods from formal semantics with compositional assembly of sentence/discourse meanings rooted in first obtaining a syntactic parse, e.g., Copestake et al. (2006), Bos (2008), Butler (2015a), and Mineshima et al (2015). Systems that natively produce Penman representations include the growing number of systems trained on the sembanks of Abstract Meaning Representation (AMR; Banarescu et al., 2013), e.g., Flanigan et al. (2014), Artzi et al. (2015), and Pust et al. (2015).

For generation from Penman representations, there is currently the Nitrogen system (Langkilde and Knight, 1998). Nitrogen relies on a statistical component to filter results generated from a base system with phrase structure like rules. Other generation systems typically start from representations of

Proceedings of the 2nd Workshop on Semantics-Driven Machine Translation, pages 1–9,
San Diego, California, June 16, 2016.

argument structure or quasi-logical forms, e.g., Alshawi (1992) and Humphreys et al (2001).

The generation of this paper builds on Butler (2015b), in that a series of transformations are followed to construct parsed trees. Trees constructed will conform to the Penn Parsed Corpus of Modern British English (PPCMBE; Kroch et al., 2010), with the yield (i.e. words) producing target sentences of English. This scheme is similar to the Penn Treebank scheme (Bies et al., 1995), but with more consistency in the projection of phrase structure (following X-bar theory; Chomsky, 1970) and handling of coordination, while clause structure is generally flat since VP occurs only with coordination.

An implementation of the generation of this paper is available from `http://www.compling.jp/generation`. The assumed engine to transform trees is provided by tsurgeon (Levy and Andrew, 2006). This works with tsurgeon scripts that contain patterns with associated actions. Patterns describe tree structure with the tree description language of tgrep (Pito, 1994) and actions transform the tree, e.g., moving, adjoining, copying or deleting auxiliary trees or relabelling nodes. Alternative programs to transform trees with scripts are CorpusSearch (Randall, 2009) and TTT (Purtee and Schubert, 2012).

3 A sketch of the generation procedure

This section sketches generation of a canonical sentence with a transitive verb:

(1) Girls see a boy.

A typical Davidsonian meaning representation for (1) is as follows:

```
∃ EVENT[3] PERSON[2] PERSONS[1]
(girls(PERSONS[1]) ∧ boy(PERSON[2])
∧ see(EVENT[3], PERSONS[1],
PERSON[2]))
```

With information for argument roles ('`:ARG0`' and '`:ARG1`') sourced from the arity of the '`see`' predicate, the same content converted to a Penman representation is as follows:

```
( EVENT-3 / see
      :ARG0 ( PERSONS-1 / girls)
      :ARG1 ( PERSON-2 / boy))
```

Already the Penman notation provides a base for growing tree structure:

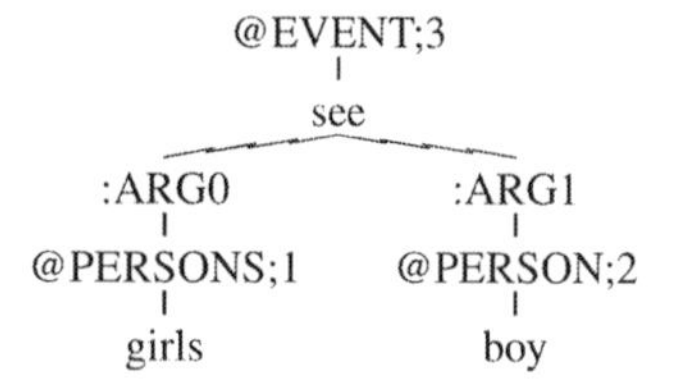

Clause structure is built by adjoining VBP, VP and IP layers to nodes beginning with '@EVENT'.

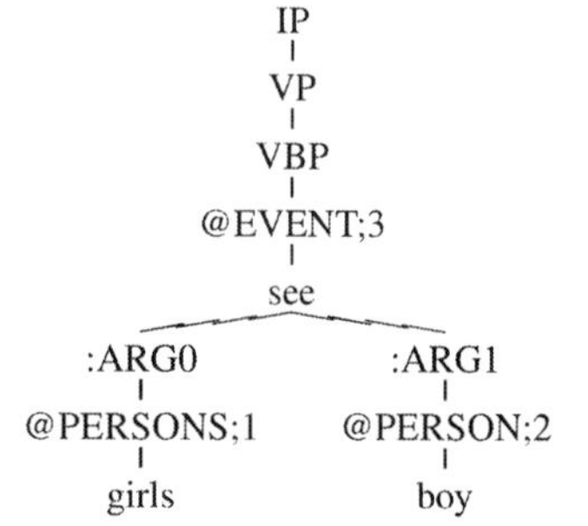

Next, arguments of what has been made the main predicate are moved to populate the clause, with '`:ARG1`' as the object inside VP, while '`:ARG0`' creates the subject outside VP.

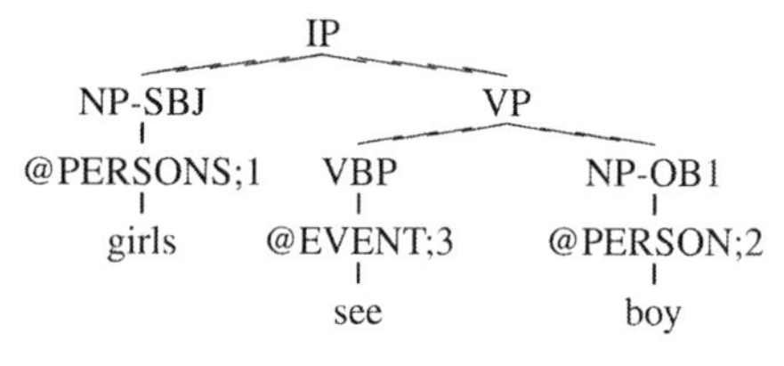

With arguments in place, it is safe to remove the VP layer and type the clause as IP-MAT (matrix clause), as well as add punctuation. Entity information is retained with BIND, which also contributes to the projection of noun part-of-speech tags (N; singular vs. NS; plural).

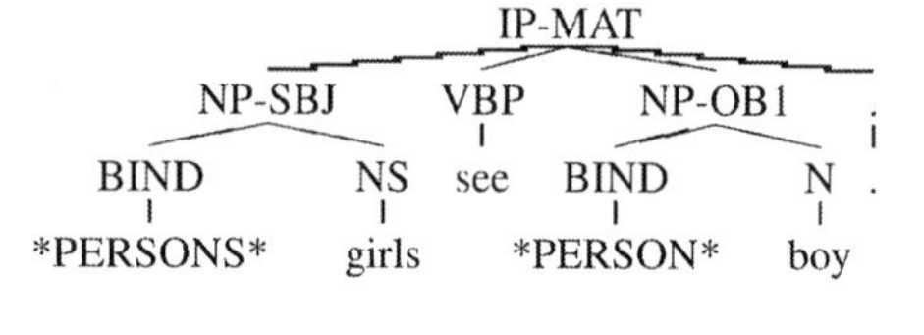

Noun phrases are left bare when indefinite, with the assumption that further post-processing might add an indefinite determiner (*a* or *an*) when the noun head is singular.

4 Different constructions

This section is concerned with how the make up of a meaning representation can determine generation of particular English language constructions as PPCMBE trees, with both meaning representation content and how the content is packaged influencing output.

4.1 Passivisation

With ':ARG0' missing, but ':ARG1' present, the content of ':ARG1' can be taken to form the grammatical subject to create a passive clause with the verb tag altered to VAG (passive participle) and BEP (present tense copula) added.

(2) A boy is seen.

```
∃ EVENT[2] PERSON[1] (boy(PERSON[1])
∧ seen(EVENT[2], _, PERSON[1]))
```

```
( EVENT-2 / seen
      :ARG1 ( PERSON-1 / boy))
```

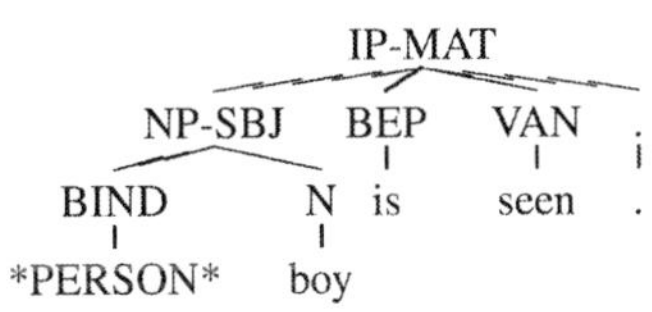

4.2 Expletive it

If there is no core argument (':ARG0', ':ARG1', or ':ARG2') then expletive *it* should be created to fulfil the grammatical subject role.

(3) It rained on Monday.

```
∃ EVENT[1] (past(EVENT[1]) ∧
rained(EVENT[1]) ∧ on(EVENT[1]) =
DATE[Monday])
```

```
( EVENT-1 / rained
      :MOD ( mod-1 / past)
      :ON ( DATE-Monday / DATE
              :name ( n-2 / name
                      :op1 "Monday")))
```

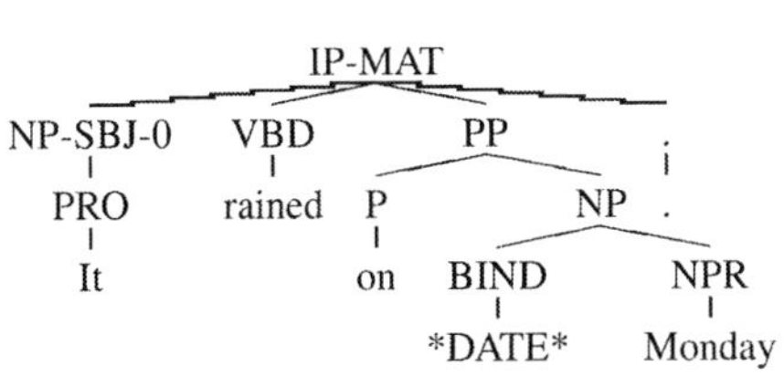

This example also demonstrates creation of a PP adjunct from an ':ON' argument, as well as the effect of past tense information altering the verb tag to VBD (past tense verb).

4.3 Existential construction

Another variation in clause construction occurs when the predicate is the copula and there is no ':ARG1', but ':ARG0' is present. This triggers creation of a *there* subject that is coindexed with the contribution of ':ARG0' captured as a noun phrase that immediately follows the copula.

(4) There is a happy laughing boy.

```
∃ ATTRIB[3] ATTRIB[2] EVENT[4]
PERSON[1] (
 happy(ATTRIB[2]) ∧
  laughing(ATTRIB[3]) ∧
is_boy_ATTRIBUTE(PERSON[1],
ATTRIB[3]) ∧ is_boy_ATTRIBUTE(PERSON[1],
ATTRIB[2]) ∧ copula(EVENT[4],
PERSON[1]))
```

```
( EVENT-4 / copula
    :ARG0 ( PERSON-1 / boy
     :ATTRIBUTE ( ATTRIB-3 / laughing)
     :ATTRIBUTE ( ATTRIB-2 / happy)))
```

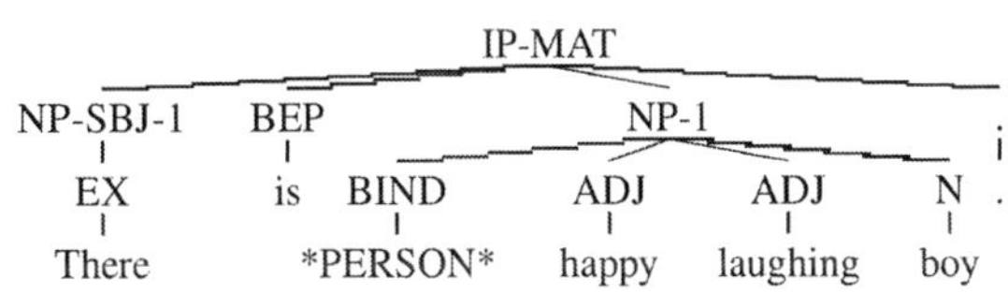

4.4 Discourse

A discourse is created when there is content for two or more clauses that are conjuncts of multi-sentence in the Penman representation.

(5) A boy is happy. He laughs.

```
∃ PERSON[3] EVENT[2] EVENT[4]
PERSON[1] (boy(PERSON[1]) ∧ PERSON[3]
= PERSON[1] ∧ copula_happy(EVENT[2],
PERSON[1]) ∧ laughs(EVENT[4],
PERSON[3]))
```

The presence of the equative link 'PERSON[3] = PERSON[1]' is a sufficient clue when converting from the Davidsonian predicate language formula to create conjuncts conjoined with `multi-sentence`.

```
( CONJ-1 / multi-sentence
       :snt1 ( EVENT-2 / copula_happy
               :ARG0 ( PERSON-1 / boy))
       :snt2 ( EVENT-4 / laughs
               :ARG0 PERSON-1))
```

With there being multiple argument roles for the same entity in distinct conjuncts, it should be the first instance in the Penman representation that is populated with information about the entity, e.g., `(PERSON-1 / boy)`, while subsequent instances are bare references, e.g., `PERSON-1`. It is such a bare reference that leads to the creation of a pronoun with the generated output.

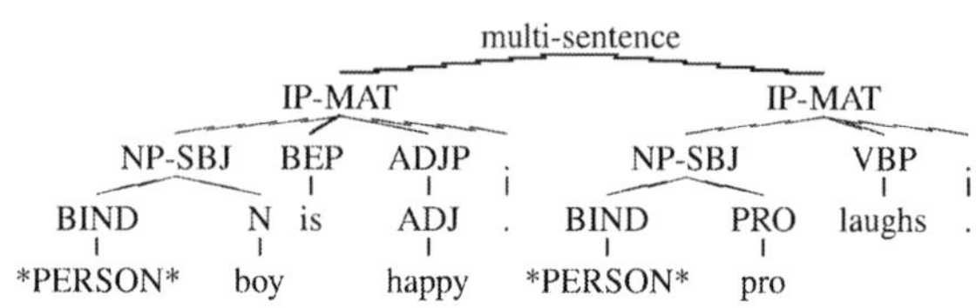

4.5 VP coordination

A relation projecting a label beginning `CONJ` is a relation of coordination. Such a relation name that is not `multi-sentence` is the foundation for forming intra sentential coordination. If the content for arguments that become subjects is shared between conjuncts then VP coordination is established to share the same subject.

(6) A boy is happy and laughs.

```
∃ EVENT[2] EVENT[3]
PERSON[1] (boy(PERSON[1]) ∧
CONJ_and(copula_happy(EVENT[2],
PERSON[1]), laughs(EVENT[3],
PERSON[1])))
```

```
( CONJ-4 / and
       :op1 ( EVENT-2 / copula_happy
               :ARG0 ( PERSON-1 / boy))
       :op2 ( EVENT-3 / laughs
               :ARG0 PERSON-1))
```

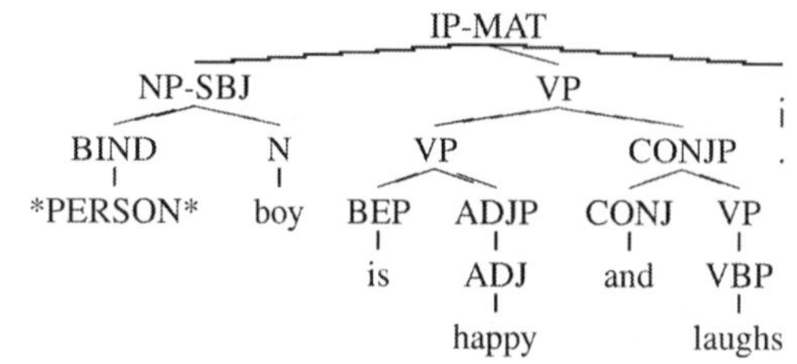

If there are other shared entities between conjuncts formed with the same argument role, then they are projected outside the VP layer, typically to the left, but to the right when the argument role is '`:ARG1`' and the verbs are active (also have '`:ARG0`' arguments), or when the argument is heavy, e.g., containing many terminal nodes.

4.6 Adverbial clause

A binary relation projecting a label beginning `CND` (conditional) or `CRD` (coordinating relation) creates an adverbial clause from the first conjunct, with the relation name forming a subordinate conjunction (e.g., *if*, *when*, *unless*, *although*, *because*) that introduces the adverbial clause to a containing clause formed from the content of the second conjunct. If the same entity fills arguments in distinct conjuncts, it should be the instance in what will form the adjunct clause that is populated with information about the entity, while subsequent instances are bare references, with bare references leading to the creation of pronouns. This is similar to the treatment of bare references when there is a `multi-sentence` relation creating discourse (see section 4.4).

(7) Because a boy is happy he laughs.

```
∃ PERSON[3] EVENT[2] EVENT[4]
PERSON[1] (
 boy(PERSON[1]) ∧
  PERSON[3] = he{PERSON[1]} ∧
CRD_Because(copula_happy(EVENT[2],
PERSON[1]), laughs(EVENT[4],
PERSON[3])))
```

```
( CRD-5 / Because
       :op1 ( EVENT-2 / copula_happy
               :ARG0 ( PERSON-1 / boy))
       :op2 ( EVENT-4 / laughs
               :ARG0 PERSON-1))
```

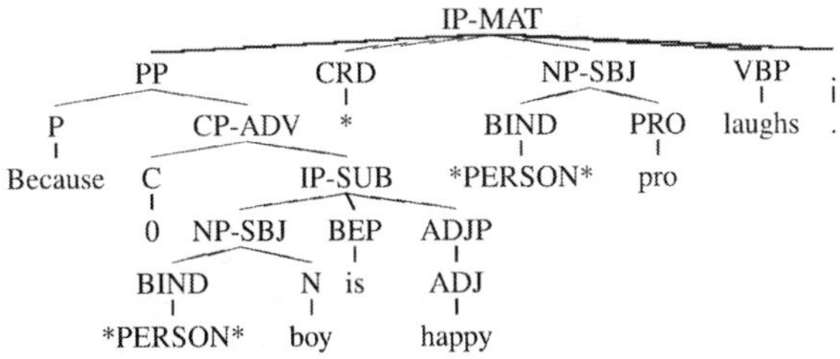

4.7 Participal clause

Instead of an adverbial clause being created from the first conjunct of a binary relation projecting a label beginning `CND` or `CRD`, a participal clause with a controlled subject is created when there is a bare reference for the '`:ARG0`' of the first conjunct that is coreferential with the content of a core argument ('`:ARG0`', '`:ARG1`' or '`:ARG2`') of the second conjunct.

(8) If laughing a boy is happy.

```
∃ EVENT[2] EVENT[3]
PERSON[1] (boy(PERSON[1]) ∧
CND_If(laughing(EVENT[2], PERSON[1]),
copula_happy(EVENT[3], PERSON[1])))
```

```
( CND-4 / If
    :op1 ( EVENT-2 / laughing
          :ARG0 PERSON-1)
    :op2 ( EVENT-3 / copula_happy
          :ARG0 ( PERSON-1 / boy)))
```

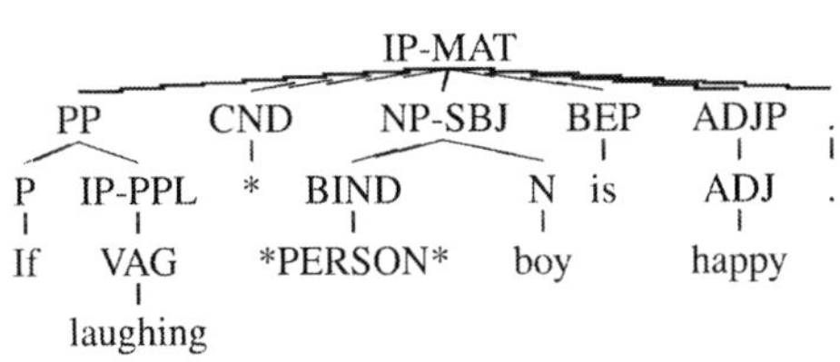

4.8 Purpose clause

A to-infinitive clause can function as an adverbial expressing ideas of purpose or outcome. The content for such a clause falls under a '`:PRP`' tag, while inside there is '`:ARG0`' containing a bare reference coreferential with (i.e., controlled by) the content of the '`:ARG0`' of the containing clause. This creates a subjectless IP-INF-PRP projection containing `(TO to)` and a non-finite verb (`VB`).

(9) To impress a girl a boy laughs.

```
∃ PRP[2] EVENT[4] EVENT[5] PERSON[3]
PERSON[1] (
 boy(PERSON[1]) ∧
  girl(PERSON[3]) ∧
   is_FACT_THAT(PRP[2],
impress(EVENT[4], PERSON[1],
PERSON[3])) ∧
    laughs(EVENT[5], PERSON[1]) ∧
PRP(EVENT[5]) = PRP[2])
```

```
( EVENT-5 / laughs
   :ARG0 ( PERSON-1 / boy)
   :PRP ( EVENT-4 / impress
          :ARG0 PERSON-1
          :ARG1 ( PERSON-3 / girl)))
```

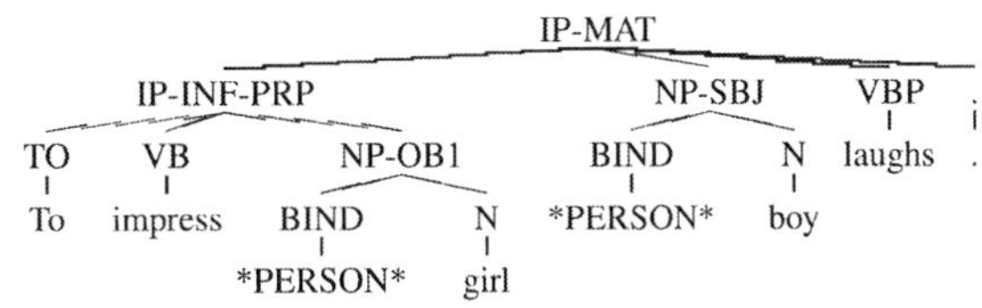

4.9 Infinitive clause with long distance dependency

Content for an embedded to-infinitive clause falls under a '`:TOCOMP`' tag, while inside there is '`:ARG0`' containing a bare reference coreferential with (i.e., controlled by) the content of the '`:ARG2`' if present, or alternatively '`:ARG1`' if present, or alternatively '`:ARG0`' of the containing clause. This creates a subjectless IP-INF projection containing `(TO to)` and a non-finite predicate.

(10) What might the boy think to do?

```
∃ ATTRIB[2] EVENT[4] EVENT[3]
PERSON[1] (
 the(ATTRIB[2]) ∧
  is_boy_definite(PERSON[1],
ATTRIB[2]) ∧
   QUEST(MD_might(think_TOCOMP(EVENT[3],
PERSON[1], do(EVENT[4], PERSON[1],
ENTITY[penman2-unknown])))))
```

```
( EVENT-3 / think
   :domain-of ( QUEST-6 / QUEST)
   :domain-of ( MD-5 / might)
   :ARG0 ( PERSON-1 / boy
     :DEFINITE ( ATTRIB-2 / the))
   :TOCOMP ( EVENT-4 / do
```

```
      :ARG0 PERSON-1
      :ARG1 ( ENTITY_UNK-2 /
penman-unknown)))
```

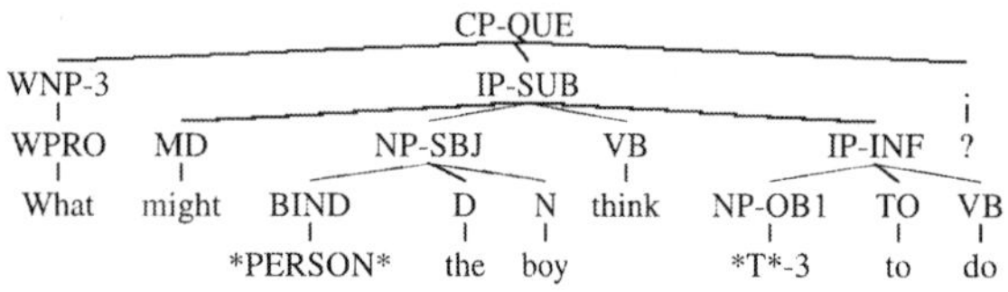

The example also illustrates how a long distance dependency is established with ‘`:ARG1 (ENTITY_UNK-2 / penman-unknown)`’ forming the foundation for an object noun phrase trace (`NP-OB1 *T*-3`) that is coindexed with a WH-phrase (`WNP-3 (WPRO What)`) that is placed as the highest constituent of the first commanding question scope marker: ‘`:domain-of (QUEST-6 / QUEST)`’.

4.10 Embedded clause with long distance dependency

An embedded clause rather than a to-infinitive is established with clause content placed under ‘`:THAT`’. Inside the content for the embedded clause, bare references form foundations for pronouns.

(11) What might the boy think that he will do?

```
∃ PERSON[4] ATTRIB[2] EVENT[5]
EVENT[3] PERSON[1] (
 the(ATTRIB[2]) ∧
  is_boy_definite(PERSON[1],
ATTRIB[2]) ∧
   PERSON[4] = he{PERSON[1]} ∧
    QUEST(MD_might(think_THAT(EVENT[3],
PERSON[1], MD_will(do(EVENT[5],
PERSON[4], ENTITY[penman2-unknown]))))))
```

```
( EVENT-3 / think
    :domain-of ( QUEST-9 / QUEST)
    :domain-of ( MD-8 / might)
    :ARG0 ( PERSON-1 / boy
        :DEFINITE ( ATTRIB-2 / the))
    :THAT ( EVENT-5 / do
        :domain-of ( MD-7 / will)
        :ARG0 PERSON-1
        :ARG1 ( ENTITY_UNK-2 /
penman-unknown)))
```

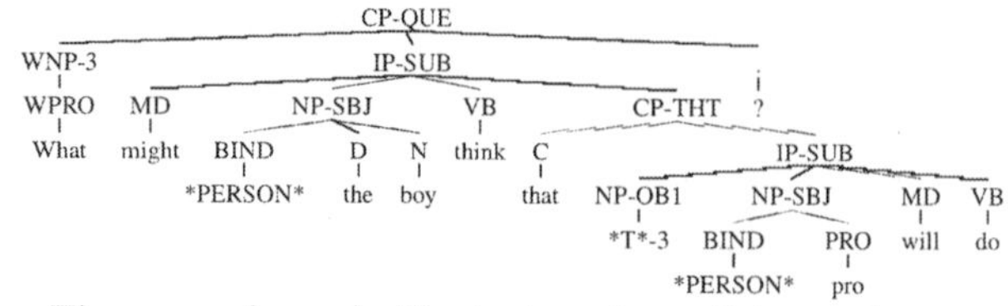

The example again illustrates a long distance dependency established out of the embedding.

4.11 Embedded question

Having the scope marker for a question local to an embedded clause results in an embedded question.

(12) A boy wonders what he will do.

```
∃ PERSON[3] EVENT[4] EVENT[2]
PERSON[1] (
 boy(PERSON[1]) ∧
  PERSON[3] = he{PERSON[1]} ∧
   wonders_THAT(EVENT[2], PERSON[1],
QUEST(MD_will(do(EVENT[4], PERSON[3],
ENTITY[penman2-unknown])))))
```

```
( EVENT-2 / wonders
   :ARG0 ( PERSON-1 / boy)
   :THAT ( EVENT-4 / do
        :domain-of ( QUEST-8 / QUEST)
        :domain-of ( MD-7 / will)
        :ARG0 PERSON-1
        :ARG1 ( ENTITY_UNK-2 /
penman-unknown)))
```

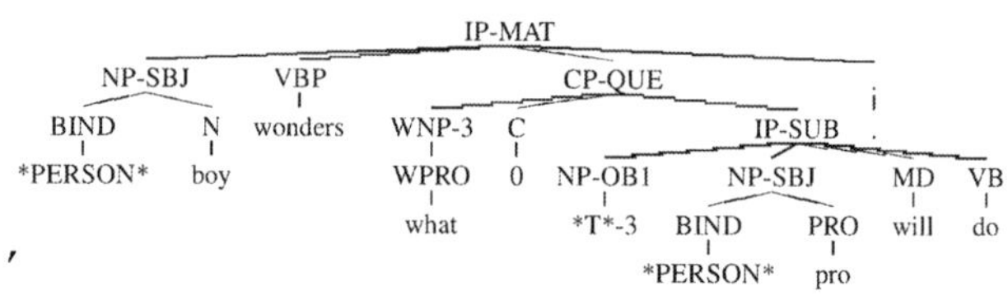

Together with the examples of section 4.9 and 4.10, this demonstrates how it is not enough for a meaning representation to mark a WH question with `penman-unknown` alone, but that scope marking the level of structure to place a fronted WH phrase is also vital.

4.12 Small clause

Small clauses are embedded clauses that occur with the absence of a finite verb.

(13) A plan to laugh makes a boy happy.

Lack of a finite verb is reflected by creation of a dummy 'EVENT' predicate that connects the subject *a boy* to the *happy* attribute in the following Davidsonian formula:

```
∃ ATTRIB[5] PERSON[4] ENTITY[1]
EVENT[2] EVENT[6] EVENT[3] (
 is_plan_TOCOMP(ENTITY[1],
laugh(EVENT[2])) ∧
 boy(PERSON[4]) ∧ happy(ATTRIB[5]) ∧
 makes_TOCOMP(EVENT[3], ENTITY[1],
EVENT(EVENT[6], PERSON[4],
ATTRIB[5])))
```

```
( EVENT-3 / makes
  :ARG0 ( ENTITY-1 / plan
     :TOCOMP ( EVENT-2 / laugh))
  :TOCOMP ( EVENT-6 / EVENT
     :ATTRIBUTE ( ATTRIB-5 / happy)
     :ARG0 ( PERSON-4 / boy)))
```

This leads to projection of an IP-SMC embedded clause with no verb/copula creation.

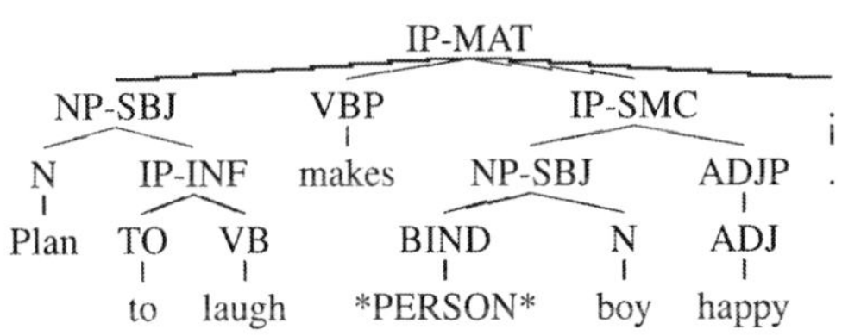

This example also illustrates creation of a nominal with an infinitive clause embedding, triggered by 'TOCOMP'.

4.13 Relative clause

The example of this section demonstrates creation of a relative clause with a long distance dependency:

(14) Every boy that a girl says is happy laughs.

There is nothing overt to signal a relative clause with the Davidsonian formula:

```
∃ ATTRIB[2] EVENT[6] EVENT[5] EVENT[7]
PERSON[4] PERSON[1] (
 every(ATTRIB[2]) ∧
  girl(PERSON[4]) ∧
   says_THAT(EVENT[5], PERSON[4],
copula_happy(EVENT[6], PERSON[1]))
∧ is_boy_QUANTIFIER(PERSON[1],
ATTRIB[2]) ∧
    laughs(EVENT[7], PERSON[1]))
```

But a base for realising a relative clause does emerge when there is conversion to Penman notation:

```
( EVENT-7 / laughs
  :ARG0 ( PERSON-1 / boy
   :QUANTIFIER ( ATTRIB-2 / every)
   :ARG0-of ( EVENT-6 / copula_happy
      :THAT-of ( EVENT-5 / says
        :ARG0 ( PERSON-4 / girl)))))
```

A key requirement for Penman notation is to connect all content around a single rooted node. This privileged node will typically form the main predicate following generation. While not necessary for being a Davidsonian forumla, a convention can be followed to place such a privileged predicate as the most right-side predicate of the formula (so, 'laughs' of the example). Connection to this single rooted predicate is possible by folding Penman material around inverse roles (signalled by ending a role name with '-of') which serves to compact the long distance dependency of the relative clause.

Generation consists of unfolding the dependency, so taking '-of' content and reintegrating the content with clausal embedded structure:

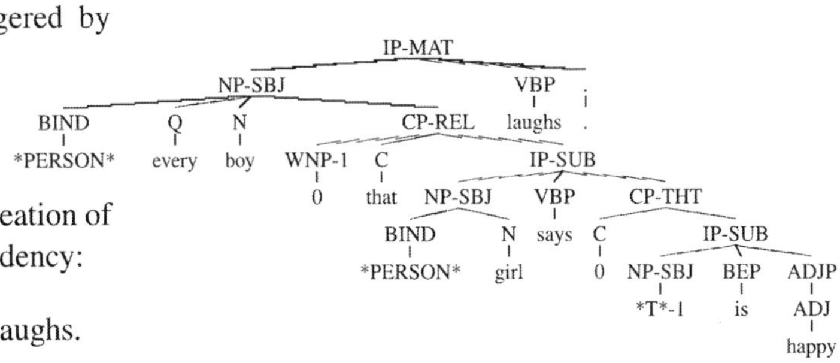

4.14 It cleft

As a final example, consider generation of an it cleft:

(15) It is the happy boy that laughs.

Such a cleft sentence leads to the presence of a copula predicate that connects 'ARG1' content to an 'ARG0' entity that, with conversion to Penman notation, is given a dummy 'ENTITY' head and is inversed linked to material sufficient to create a clause:

```
∃ ATTRIB[3] ATTRIB[2] ENTITY[4]
EVENT[6] EVENT[7] PERSON[1] (
 the(ATTRIB[2]) ∧
  happy(ATTRIB[3]) ∧
   is_boy_ATTRIBUTE(PERSON[1],
ATTRIB[3]) ∧ is_boy_definite(PERSON[1],
ATTRIB[2]) ∧
    laughs(EVENT[6], ENTITY[4])
∧ copula(EVENT[7], ENTITY[4],
PERSON[1]))
```

```
( EVENT-7 / copula
  :ARG0 ( ENTITY-4 / ENTITY
    :ARG0-of ( EVENT-6 / laughs))
  :ARG1 ( PERSON-1 / boy
    :DEFINITE ( ATTRIB-2 / the)
    :ATTRIBUTE ( ATTRIB-3 / happy)))
```

This leads to generation of the following tree:

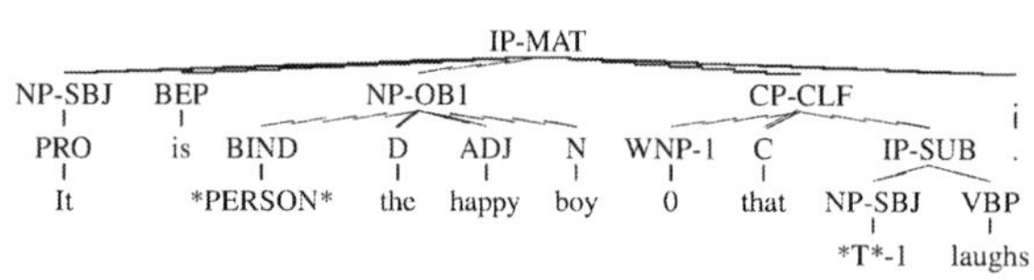

Internally, the it cleft has the same structure as a relative clause, but externally, it is a daughter of IP.

5 Conclusion

This paper has focused on the generation of various English language constructions from meaning representations. Starting as Davidsonian predicate language formulas converted to Penman representations, meaning representations were changed to trees to form the basis for generation that proceeds with successive tree structure changes.

Language generation raises the issue of how to choose between the many ways a language offers to present content. The novel contribution of this paper has been to demonstrate how there can be a significant role for meaning representations to play in influencing the selection of grammatical constructions with the arrangement of information content, notably, handling distinctions of clause type as well as the choice between discourse, or (VP) coordination, or projection of an adverbial clause, or participial clause, or creation of a small clause, or infinitive embedding, or finite embedding, or relative clause, or it cleft. This has simplified what it takes to create a generation component capable of rich, varied and natural output, but also, most importantly, this will ensure there is preservation of meaning.

Preserving meaning is an issue since the constructions on display should rarely be conflated, with, e.g., variation in the placement of noun phrase restriction material, or coordinate material, or adjunct material, or embedded material typically giving differences in meaning. Arguably, results of this paper come at the cost of making the creation of meaning representations a more complex task. In this regard, the approach is especially suitable as a component of a machine translation system with meaning representations as the level for language transfer, since the source language of translation will offer rich information to drive how the content of a derived meaning representation is presented.

Acknowledgements

This paper has benefitted from the comments of three anonymous reviewers, as well as discussions with Pascual Martínez-Gómez, Masaaki Nagata and Kei Yoshimoto, all of which is very gratefully acknowledged. This research is supported by the Japan Society for the Promotion of Science (JSPS), Research Project Number: 15K02469.

References

Hiyan Alshawi. 1992. *The Core Language Engine*. Cambridge, Mass.: MIT Press.

Yoav Artzi, Kenton Lee, and Luke Zettlemoyer. 2015. Broad-coverage CCG semantic parsing with AMR. In *Proceedings of the 2015 Conference on Empirical Methods in Natural Language Processing*, page 1699–1710. Lisbon, Portugal.

L. Banarescu, C. Bonial, S. Cai, M. Georgescu, K. Griffitt, U. Hermjakob, K. Knight, P. Koehn, M. Palmer, and N. Schneider. 2013. Abstract Meaning Representation for Sembanking. In *Proceedings of the 7th Linguistic Annotation Workshop and Interoperability with Discourse*, pages 178–186.

Ann Bies, Mark Ferguson, Karen Katz, and Robert MacIntyre. 1995. Bracketing guidelines for Treebank II style Penn Treebank project. Tech. Rep. MS-CIS-95-06, LINC LAB 281, University of Pennsylvania Computer and Information Science Department.

Johan Bos. 2008. Wide-coverage semantic analysis with Boxer. In J. Bos and R. Delmonte, eds., *Semantics in Text Processing. STEP 2008 Conference Proceedings*, Research in Computational Semantics, pages 277–286. College Publications.

Alastair Butler. 2015a. *Linguistic Expressions and Semantic Processing: A Practical Approach*. Heidelberg: Springer-Verlag.

Alastair Butler. 2015b. Round-trips with meaning stopovers. In *Proceedings of the 1st Workshop on Semantics-Driven Statistical Machine Translation*, pages 1–10. Beijing, China: Association for Computational Linguistics.

Noam Chomsky. 1970. Remarks on nominalization. In R. Jacobs and P. Rosenbaum, eds., *Readings in English Transformational Grammar*, pages 184–221. Waltham, MA: Ginn.

Ann Copestake, Dan Flickinger, Carl Pollard, and Ivan A. Sag. 2006. Minimala Recursion Semantics: an introduction. *Research on Language and Computation* 3(4):281–332.

Donald Davidson. 1967. The logical form of action sentences. In N. Rescher, ed., *The Logic of Decision and Action*. Pittsburgh: University of Pittsburgh Press. Reprinted in: D. Davidson, 1980. *Essays on Actions and Events*. Claredon Press, Oxford, pages 105–122.

Jeffrey Flanigan, Sam Thomson, Jaime Carbonell, Chris Dyer, and Noah A. Smith. 2014. A discriminative graph-based parser for the abstract meaning representation. In *Proc. of the ACL 2014*.

Kevin Humphreys, Mike Calcagno, and David Weise. 2001. Reusing a statistical language model for generation. In *Proceedings of the 8th European workshop on Natural Language Generation - Volume 8*, pages 1–6. Stroudsburg, PA: Association for Computational Linguistics.

Anthony Kroch, Beatrice Santorini, and Ariel Diertani. 2010. *The Penn-Helsinki Parsed Corpus of Modern British English (PPCMBE)*. Department of Linguistics, University of Pennsylvania. CD-ROM, second edition, (http://www.ling.upenn.edu/hist-corpora).

Fred Landman. 2000. *Events and Plurality: The Jerusalem Lectures*. Dordrecht: Kluwer Academic Publishers.

Irene Langkilde and Kevin Knight. 1998. Generation that exploits corpus-based statistical knowledge. In *Proceedings of the ACL/COLING-98*. Montreal, Quebéc.

Roger Levy and Galen Andrew. 2006. Tregex and tsurgeon: tools for querying and manipulating tree data structure. In *5th International conference on Language Resources and Evaluation*.

Christian Matthiessen and John A Bateman. 1991. *Text generation and systemic-functional linguistics: experiences from English and Japanese*. Pinter Publishers.

Koji Mineshima, Pascual Martínez-Gómez, Yusuke Miyao, and Daisuke Bekki. 2015. Higher-order logical inference with compositional semantics. In *Proceedings of the 2015 Conference on Empirical Methods in Natural Language Processing (EMNLP 2015)*, pages 2055–2061. Lisbon, Portugal.

Terence Parsons. 1990. *Events in the Semantics of English*. Cambridge: MIT Press.

Richard Pito. 1994. tgrepdoc - documentation for tgrep.

A. Purtee and Lenhart K. Schubert. 2012. TTT: A tree transduction language for syntactic and semantic processing. In *EACL 2012 Workshop on Applications of Tree Automata Techniques in Natural Language Processing (ATANLP 2012)*. Avignon, France.

Michael Pust, Ulf Hermjakob, Kevin Knight, Daniel Marcu, and Jonathan May. 2015. Parsing english into abstract meaning representation using syntax-based machine translation. In *Proceedings of the 2015 Conference on Empirical Methods in Natural Language Processing*, pages 1143–1154. Lisbon, Portugal.

Beth Randall. 2009. CorpusSearch 2 Users Guide. (http://corpussearch.sourceforge.net/CS-manual/Contents.html).

Extending Phrase-Based Translation with Dependencies by Using Graphs

Liangyou Li and **Andy Way** and **Qun Liu**
ADAPT Centre, School of Computing
Dublin City University, Ireland
{liangyouli,away,qliu}@computing.dcu.ie

Abstract

In this paper, we propose a graph-based translation model which takes advantage of discontinuous phrases. The model segments a graph which combines bigram and dependency relations into subgraphs and produces translations by combining translations of these subgraphs. Experiments on Chinese–English and German–English tasks show that our system is significantly better than the phrase-based model. By explicitly modeling the graph segmentation, our system gains further improvement.

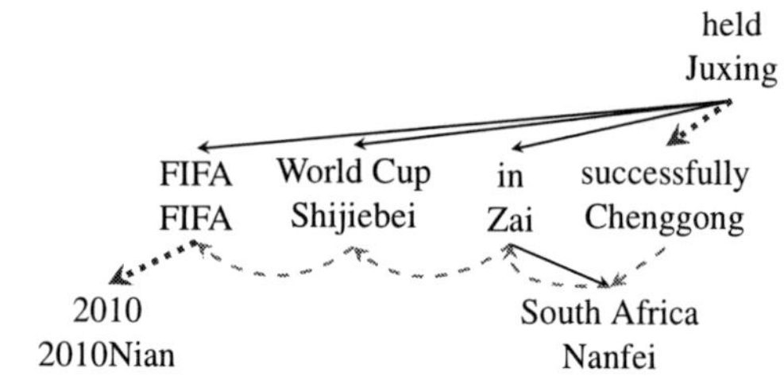

Figure 1: An example of constructing a graph for a Chinese sentence. Each node includes a Chinese word and its English meaning. Dashed red lines are bigram relations. Dark lines are dependency relations. Dotted blue lines are shared by bigram and dependency relations.

1 Introduction

One significant weakness of conventional phrase-based (PB) models (Koehn et al., 2003) is that it only uses continuous phrases and thus cannot learn generalizations, such as French *ne. . . pas* to English *not* (Galley and Manning, 2010). Although using tree structures is believed to be a promising way to solve this problem by learning either translation patterns (Chiang, 2005; Galley et al., 2004; Liu et al., 2006) or treelets (Menezes and Quirk, 2005; Quirk et al., 2005; Xiong et al., 2007), handling non-syntactic phrases is still a big challenge.

In this paper, we propose a graph-based translation model which translates a graph into a string by segmenting the graph into subgraphs. Each subgraph is connected and may cover discontinuous phrases. Experiments show that our model is significantly better than the PB model. Explicitly modeling the graph segmentation further improves our system.

2 Graph-Based Translation

Our graph-based translation model extends PB translation by translating an input graph rather than a sequence to a target string, as in Equation (1):

$$p(t \mid G(s)) = \prod_{i=1}^{I} P(\bar{t}_i|G(\tilde{s}_{a_i}))d(\tilde{s}_{a_i}, \tilde{s}_{a_{i-1}}) \quad (1)$$

where $\tilde{s}$ denotes a source phrase which may be discontinuous and $G(\tilde{s})$ indicates a connected graph covering $\tilde{s}$. d is a distortion function.[1]

2.1 Building Graphs

As a more powerful and natural structure for sentence representation, a graph can model various word-relations together in a unified way. In this paper, we use graphs to combine two commonly

[1] In this paper, we use a distortion function, defined in Galley and Manning (2010), to penalize discontinuous phrases that have relatively long gaps.

Proceedings of the 2nd Workshop on Semantics-Driven Machine Translation, pages 10–12,
San Diego, California, June 16, 2016.

used relations: bigram relations and dependency relations. In this way, we can make use of both continuous and linguistic-informed discontinuous phrases as long as they are connected subgraphs. Figure 1 shows an example of a graph.

2.2 Training and Decoding

Different from the PB model, the basic translation units in our model are subgraphs. During training, we extract subgraph–phrase pairs instead of phrase pairs on parallel graph-string sentences associated with word alignments.

Our graph-based decoder is based on beam search and generates hypotheses (partial translations) from left to right. Each hypothesis can be extended by translating an uncovered source subgraph. The translation process ends when no untranslated words remain.

2.3 Graph Segmentation Model

We define a set of sparse features to explicitly model a graph segmentation. Given previous subgraphs, for each node in a current subgraph, we extract the following features:

$$\begin{Bmatrix} n.w \\ n.c \end{Bmatrix} \times \begin{Bmatrix} n'.w \\ n'.c \end{Bmatrix} \times \begin{Bmatrix} C \\ P \\ H \end{Bmatrix} \times \begin{Bmatrix} in \\ out \end{Bmatrix}$$

where $n.w$ and $n.c$ are the word and class of a current node n, and n' is a node connected to n. C, P, and H denote that n' is in the current subgraph or the last previous subgraph or other previous subgraphs, respectively. *in* and *out* denote that an edge is an in-coming edge or out-going edge of n.

In this paper we lexicalize only on the top-100 frequent words (Cherry, 2013). In addition, we group source words into 50 classes by using *mkcls*.

3 Experiments and Results

Our Chinese–English (ZH–EN) training corpus contains 1.5M+ sentence pairs from LDC. Our German–English (DE–EN) training corpus (2M+ sentence pairs) is from WMT 2014. **GBMT** is our graph-based translation system and **GSM** adds the graph segmentation model into GBMT. **DTU** extends the PB model by allowing source discontinuous phrases (Galley and Manning, 2010). All systems are implemented in Moses (Koehn et al., 2007).

System	ZH–EN		DE–EN	
	NIST04	NIST05	WMT12	WMT13
PBMT	32.8	31.4	19.6	21.9
DTU	33.4*	31.5	19.8*	22.3*
GBMT	33.7*+	31.7	19.8*	22.4*
GSM	33.8*+	32.0*+	20.3*+	22.9*+

Table 1: BLEU (Papineni et al., 2002) scores for all systems on two datasets. Each score is the average score over three MIRA (Cherry and Foster, 2012) runs (Clark et al., 2011). $*$ means a system is significantly better than PBMT at $p \leq 0.01$. $+$ means a system is significantly better than DTU at $p \leq 0.01$.

System	# Rules	
	ZH–EN	DE–EN
DTU	224M+	352M+
GBMT	99M+	153M+

Table 2: The number of rules in DTU and GBMT.

Table 1 shows our main results. Our system GBMT is better than PBMT as measured by all three metrics across all testsets. This improvement is reasonable as GBMT allows discontinuous phrases which can reduce data sparsity and handle long-distance relations (Galley and Manning, 2010).

Since phrases from syntactic structures are fewer in number but more reliable (Koehn et al., 2003), our system GBMT achieves slightly better performance than DTU but uses significantly fewer rules, as shown in Table 2. After integrating the graph segmentation model to help subgraph selection, our system (GSM) achieves significantly better BLEU than DTU on both language pairs.

4 Conclusion

In this paper, we present a graph-based translation model which extends the phrase-based model by allowing discontinuous phrases.

Acknowledgments

This research has received funding from the People Programme (Marie Curie Actions) of the European Union's Framework Programme (FP7/2007-2013) under REA grant agreement nº 317471. The ADAPT Centre for Digital Content Technology is funded under the SFI Research Centres Programme (Grant 13/RC/2106) and is co-funded under the European Regional Development Fund.

References

Colin Cherry and George Foster. 2012. Batch Tuning Strategies for Statistical Machine Translation. In *Proceedings of the 2012 Conference of the North American Chapter of the Association for Computational Linguistics: Human Language Technologies*, pages 427–436, Montreal, Canada, June.

Colin Cherry. 2013. Improved Reordering for Phrase-Based Translation using Sparse Features. In *Proceedings of the 2013 Conference of the North American Chapter of the Association for Computational Linguistics: Human Language Technologies*, pages 22–31, Atlanta, Georgia, June.

David Chiang. 2005. A Hierarchical Phrase-based Model for Statistical Machine Translation. In *Proceedings of the 43rd Annual Meeting on Association for Computational Linguistics*, pages 263–270, Ann Arbor, Michigan, June.

Jonathan H. Clark, Chris Dyer, Alon Lavie, and Noah A. Smith. 2011. Better Hypothesis Testing for Statistical Machine Translation: Controlling for Optimizer Instability. In *Proceedings of the 49th Annual Meeting of the Association for Computational Linguistics: Human Language Technologies: Short Papers - Volume 2*, pages 176–181, Portland, Oregon, June.

Michel Galley and Christopher D. Manning. 2010. Accurate Non-hierarchical Phrase-Based Translation. In *Human Language Technologies: The 2010 Annual Conference of the North American Chapter of the Association for Computational Linguistics*, pages 966–974, Los Angeles, California, June.

Michel Galley, Mark Hopkins, Kevin Knight, and Daniel Marcu. 2004. What's in a Translation Rule? In *HLT-NAACL 2004: Main Proceedings*, page 273280, Boston, Massachusetts, USA, May.

Philipp Koehn, Franz Josef Och, and Daniel Marcu. 2003. Statistical Phrase-Based Translation. In *Proceedings of the 2003 Conference of the North American Chapter of the Association for Computational Linguistics on Human Language Technology - Volume 1*, pages 48–54, Edmonton, Canada, July.

Philipp Koehn, Hieu Hoang, Alexandra Birch, Chris Callison-Burch, Marcello Federico, Nicola Bertoldi, Brooke Cowan, Wade Shen, Christine Moran, Richard Zens, Chris Dyer, Ondej Bojar, Alexandra Constantin, and Evan Herbst. 2007. Moses: Open Source Toolkit for Statistical Machine Translation. In *Proceedings of the 45th Annual Meeting of the ACL on Interactive Poster and Demonstration Sessions*, pages 177–180, Prague, Czech Republic, June.

Yang Liu, Qun Liu, and Shouxun Lin. 2006. Tree-to-string Alignment Template for Statistical Machine Translation. In *Proceedings of the 21st International Conference on Computational Linguistics and the 44th Annual Meeting of the Association for Computational Linguistics*, pages 609–616, Sydney, Australia, July.

Arul Menezes and Chris Quirk. 2005. Dependency Treelet Translation: The Convergence of Statistical and Example-Based Machine-translation? In *Proceedings of the Workshop on Example-based Machine Translation at MT Summit X*, September.

Kishore Papineni, Salim Roukos, Todd Ward, and Wei-Jing Zhu. 2002. BLEU: A Method for Automatic Evaluation of Machine Translation. In *Proceedings of the 40th Annual Meeting on Association for Computational Linguistics*, pages 311–318, Philadelphia, Pennsylvania, July.

Chris Quirk, Arul Menezes, and Colin Cherry. 2005. Dependency Treelet Translation: Syntactically Informed Phrasal SMT. In *Proceedings of the 43rd Annual Meeting of the Association for Computational Linguistics (ACL'05)*, pages 271–279, Ann Arbor, Michigan, June.

Deyi Xiong, Qun Liu, and Shouxun Lin. 2007. A Dependency Treelet String Correspondence Model for Statistical Machine Translation. In *Proceedings of the Second Workshop on Statistical Machine Translation*, pages 40–47, Prague, June.

The Naming Sharing Structure and its Cognitive Meaning in Chinese and English

Shili Ge, Rou Song
Guangdong Collaborative Innovation Center for Language Research & Service, Guangdong University of Foreign Studies, Guangzhou, China 510420

Abstract

This research puts forward two concepts, the Naming Sharing Structure (NSS) and the Naming-Telling clause (NT clause). By transforming linear text into a plane structure, we discovered five construction patterns of NT clause for the NSS. The constructions of NT clauses are order-preserving, non-transgressive, and syntactically well-formed. These features of NT clause can be explained from the point of view of cognition.

1 NT Clause and Naming Sharing Structure

Indo-European languages are verb centered in syntactical and semantic analysis, and are analyzed into SVO or verb argument structure (e.g. Pollard & Sag 1994, Dalrymple 2001, and Carnie 2013). This approach is not as suitable to Chinese since many Chinese clauses are subject- or verb-less. Moreover, basically many Chinese verbs can also function as nouns (Shen, 2013). On the other hand, Chinese is a topical language, so it is more convenient to analyze Chinese clauses from the perspective of a topic-comment structure. Topic refers here to the similar concept as used in Systemic Functional Grammar (SFL; Halliday, 1994), but "subject", the traditional term, is also used together with a few adverbial and predicative components, so the concept of topic used here is more general.

We refer to this type of topic as a 'naming'. In combination, a naming (i.e. a reference) and a 'telling', which predicates or explains the naming, comprise an NT clause. When more than one telling shares the same naming, these NT clauses actually form a naming-centered syntactical structure, which referred to as Naming Sharing Structure (NSS). The NSS is distinctively different from verb-centered structure. This study is aimed at discovering the structural patterns of NSS and discusses its cognitive meaning and applicability.

The two-dimensional schema of NSS is illustrated in Section 2, and the shape of the schema can intuitively show the formal properties of NSS. In Section 3 and 4, examples of NSS in Chinese and English texts are illustrated respectively, and their patterns of constructing NT clauses are presented. The cognitive meaning of NSS is discussed in Section 5 and a conclusion offered in section 6.

2 The Newline-Indent Schema and the Naming Sharing Structure

Example 1 (Qian Zhongshu *Fortress Besieged*)

高松年发奋办公，夙夜匪懈，精明得真是睡觉还睁着眼睛，戴着眼镜，做梦都不含糊的。摇篮也挑选得很好，在平成县乡下一个本地财主家的花园里，面溪背山。

Translation:

Kao Sung-nien worked furiously day and night without rest. He was so keen he literally slept with his eyes wide open and his glasses on, so that he was never lazy even in his dreams. The cradle had been very well chosen. It was the garden of a local millionaire, in the countryside of the P'ing-ch'eng district; it faced a stream with mountains in the

Proceedings of the 2nd Workshop on Semantics-Driven Machine Translation, pages 13–21,
San Diego, California, June 16, 2016. ©2016 Association for Computational Linguistics

background. (Translated by Jeanne Kelly and Nathan K. Mao, 2003)

This example includes the eight punctuation clauses c1-c8. A punctuation clause (P-clause) is a text segment which is separated from the surrounding context by a comma, semicolon, period, exclamation mark, or question mark (See Song, 2013). All the P-clauses in this ex-ample, except for the first one, share components from their previous P-clauses to make sense. Following each punctuation mark, a carriage-return and newline mark is inserted, so that every P-clause takes up one line. Then the clause is indented right after its shared components. The left schema in Figure 1 is called Newline-Indent Schema (NIS). It transforms linear text into two dimensional plane structure which shows intuitionally the components in the previous context of a P-clause that should be supplemented at the beginning of the P-clause.

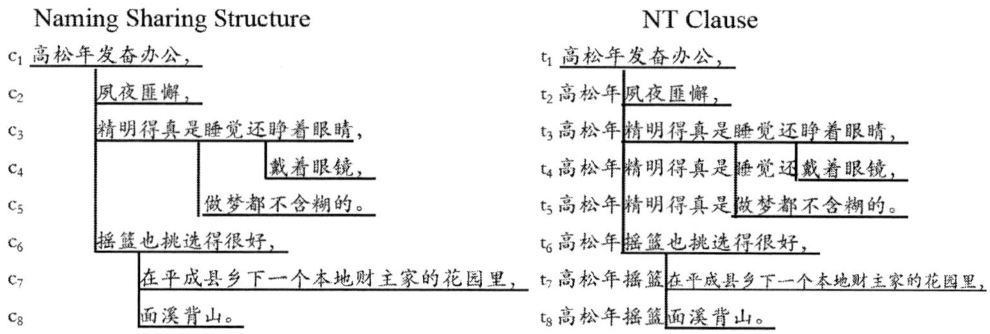

Figure 1: The Chinese Naming Sharing Structure and NT Clause illustrated with NIS.

In the right of Figure 1, the supplemented result of every P-clause is listed. They are complete naming-telling structures, referred to as NT clauses.

3 Chinese NSS and patterns constructing NT clauses

3.1 Stack Pattern

In example 1, the pattern in which NT clauses are constructed is called Stack Pattern, since the left end of every line is treated as the stack bottom and the right end as the stack top, and the construction of NT clause is exactly a process of pop and push of a stack as shown in Figure 2.

c1 高松年发奋办公 // the first P-clause c1 is in the stack initially; pop out "发奋办公"
+c2 夙夜匪懈 //the second P-clause c2 is pushed in
=t2 高松年夙夜匪懈 //get NT clause t2 of c2; pop out "夙夜匪懈"
+c3 精明得真是睡觉还睁着眼睛 //push in c3
=t3 高松年精明得真是睡觉还睁着眼睛 //get NT clause t3 of c3; pop out "睁着眼睛"
+c4 戴着眼镜 // push in c4
=t4 高松年精明得真是睡觉还戴着眼镜 //get t4; pop out "睡觉……"
+c5 做梦都不含糊的 //push in c5
=t5 高松年精明得真是做梦都不含糊的 //get t5; pop out "精明得……"
+c6 摇篮也挑选得很好 //push in c6
=t6 高松年摇篮也挑选得很好 //get t6; pop out "也挑选得很好"
+c7 在平成县乡下一个本地财主家的花园里 //push in c7
=t7 高松年摇篮在平成县乡下一个本地财主家的花园里 // get t7; pop out "在平城县……"
+c8 面溪背山 // push in c8
=t8 高松年摇篮面溪背山 // get t8

Figure 2: An iterating process of NT Clause constructed by Stack Pattern.

3.2 Back Position Pattern

Example 2 (Zhang Xianliang *Geezer Xing and his dog*)

户口不迁来，再没有个娃娃，女人迟早得回老家，

Translation:

Her Hukou is not official reregistered, and with no children, the woman will go back hometown sooner or later,

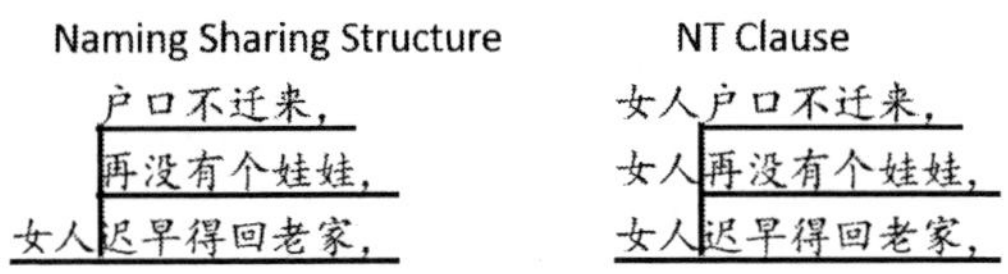

Figure 3: Back Position Pattern of Chinese.

In this example, the first two P-clauses are both lack of the subject “女人” (woman), which appears at the beginning of the third P-clause. In order to construct NT clauses of these two P-clauses, “女人” (woman) has to be supplemented based on the later context. Hence, the pattern is named Back Position Pattern.

3.3 New Branch Pattern

Example 3 (Qian Zhongshu *Fortress Besieged*)

他把带到银行里偷空看的书翻开，每个字都认识，没一句有意义。听见外面跑堂招呼客人的声音，心就直提上来。

Translation:

He opened the book he had brought to the bank to read during his spare time but not a single sentence made any sense. When he heard the waiter greeting a customer outside, his heart fluttered. (Translated by Jeanne Kelly and Nathan K. Mao, 2003)

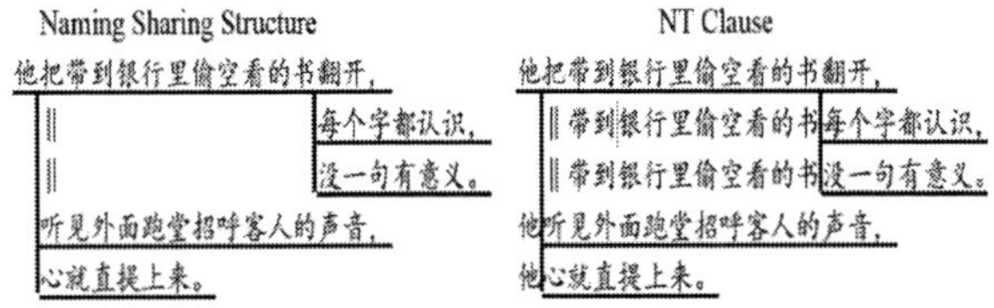

Figure 4: New Branch Pattern of Chinese.

Both P-clause 2 and 3 in the examples lack the naming “带到银行里偷看的书” (the book he had brought to the bank to read during his spare time), instead of “他把带到银行里偷看的书” (He does the book he had brought to the bank to read during his spare time). This is like placing a sluice between “他把” (He does) and “带到银行里偷看的书” (the book he had brought to the bank to read during his spare time) (the sluice is represented with mark ‖). The components on the left of the sluice is not in the naming while on the right is the naming for the following two P-clauses. This naming is like a new branch growing on a tree trunk, hence we refer to it as New Branch, and the pattern New Branch Pattern.

3.4 Influx Pattern

Example 4 (Qian Zhongshu *Fortress Besieged*)

他们都是上了年纪，有孩子的人，

Translation:

They’re older and have kids. (Translated by Jeanne Kelly and Nathan K. Mao, 2003)

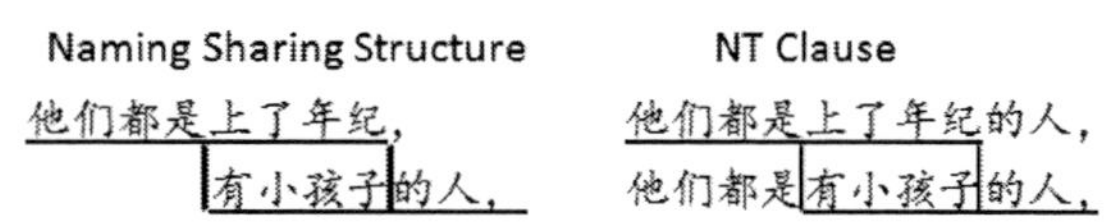

Figure 5: Influx Pattern of Chinese.

In this example, not only the second P-clause lacks a naming in its beginning, but the first P-clause also lacks an ending “的人” (person) from the tail of the second P-clause should follow it. This is just like that the utterance flow starts from “他们都是” (They all are) into two tributaries “上了年纪” (older) and “有小孩子” (have kids), then the two tributaries flow to “的人” (person). Hence we name the pattern Influx Pattern.

3.5 Enclosed Chunk Pattern

The previous patterns are based on geometrical structure. When mentioning direct quotation, the construction of NT clause needs another kind of pattern to distinguish different layers of utterance.

Example 5 (Jin Yong *The Deer and the Cauldron*)

查伊璜心想：“我连吴六奇的名字也没听见过，为何送礼于我？”当下沉吟不语。

Translation:

“I've never even heard this man's name before,” Zha thought. “Whatever should he be sending me a present for?” He remained rapt in thought and made no response. （Translated and edited by John Minford, 1999）

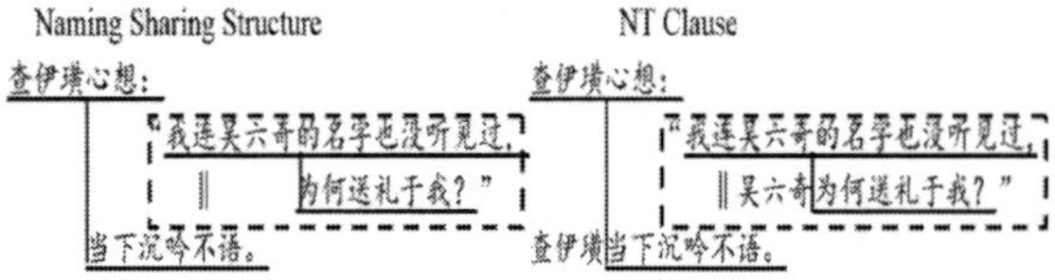

Figure 6: Enclosed Chunk Pattern of Chinese.

This example contains a direct quotation describing psychological activity. Its inside (indicated by the dotted line frame) and outside segments each form a NSS, respectively. And each of NSS constructs NT clauses according to its own pattern. Since their internal structure is enclosed from their outside contexts, we refer to this pattern as the Enclosed Chunk Pattern.

We annotated NSS for texts with different Chinese styles. Each text is annotated from beginning to end, resulting in about 40,000 NT clauses in total. We found that the five patterns of NT clause construction account for 97% of P-clause in Chinese texts.

4 The English NSS and the patterns of constructing NT clauses

4.1 English NT Clauses

Some English sentence (texts separated by period, exclamation mark, question mark) are larger, and of more complex structures than Chinese, but they still can be separated into several NT clauses, based on relationship of naming and telling. The English NT clause can be classified into an SV clause – consisting of subject and predicate –, and a non-SV clause, where the latter may consist of the following:

- antecedent+relative clause
- NP+ post-modifying nonfinite verb phrase (past participle phrase, present participle phrase and infinitive phrase)
- NP+ post-modifying declarative preposition phrase
- NP+ post-modifying adjective phrase
- NP+ post-modifying noun phrase (apposition and other explanatory NP)
- Verbal object + verbal complement

Example 6 (*Wall Street Journal*)

Documents filed with the Securities and Exchange Commission on the pending spinoff disclosed that Cray Research Inc. will withdraw the almost $ 100 million in financing it is providing the new firm if Mr. Cray leaves or if the product-design project he heads is scrapped .

The relationship of naming-telling in this long sentence can be shown in the following NIS:

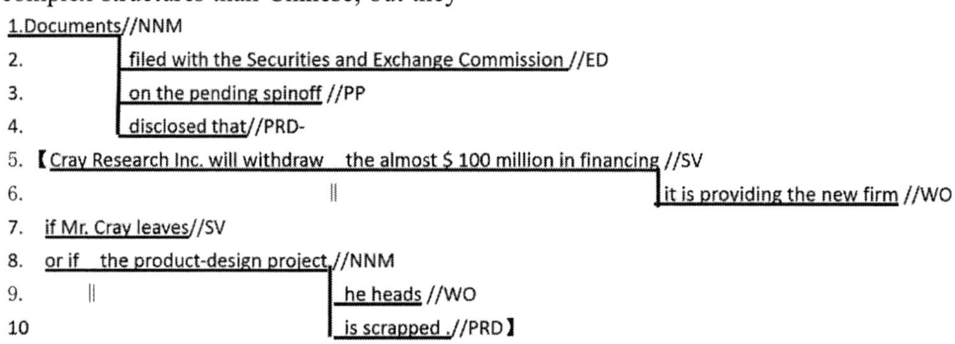

Figure 7: Naming Sharing Structure in English text.

In Example 6, the parts enclosed in the black brackets, the object clause of "disclose", is an enclosed chunk. The token on the right side of double slash, which is at the right end of each line, represents the type of this line, which is naming, telling, or NT clause. They stand for:

- NNM：NP as naming
- ED：past participle phrase as telling
- PP：preposition phrase as telling
- PRD： the predicate in SV structure as telling
- PRD-： the predicate in SV structure as telling, but lacks object clause
- SV：SV structure as NT clause
- WO：relative clause as telling, antecedent as object of the relative clause

All the above categories of telling can be supplemented by naming just as in Chinese, which come exactly from the line right above:

1.Documents//NNM
2.Documents filed with the Securities and Exchange Commission //ED
3.Documents on the pending spinoff //PP
4.Documents disclosed that//PRD-
5. 【Cray Research Inc.will withdraw the almost $ 100 million in financing //SV
6. ‖ the almost $ 100 million in financing it is providing the new firm //WO
7. if Mr. Cray leaves//SV
8. or if the product-design project //NNM
9. ‖ the product-design project he heads //WO
10 or if the product-design project is scrapped .//PRD】

Figure 8: NT clauses in English text.

4.2 Patterns constructing the English NT clause

Using the texts from the Wall Street Journal, we have built an English corpus containing nearly 2,000 English sentences, which were separated into about 6,000 NT clauses. These NT clauses are constructed through the Stack Pattern, the Back Position Pattern, the New Branch Pattern, the Influx Pattern, and the Enclosed Chunk Pattern. These five patterns account for more than 99% of the NT clauses in the corpus. In Figure 8, each line is an NT clause, except that line 1 and line 8 are only namings. Line 5 and line 7 are SV type of NT clauses; line 2, line 3, line 4, and line 10 are constructed according to the Stack Pattern, whereas line 6 and line 9 to the New Branch Pattern; from line 5 to 10, there is an Enclosed Chunk. In the following examples, NT clauses constructed through the Back Position Pattern and the Influx Pattern are illustrated.

Example 7 (*Wall Street Journal*)

As being so fragile and minute, they will require special robotic handling equipment .

The naming-telling relationship in this text can be illustrated by the NIS:

As being so fragile and minute
they will require special robotic handling equipment .

they as being so fragile and minute
they will require special robotic handling equipment .

Figure 9: The Back Position Pattern in English.

In this figure, the preposition phrase in line 1 should take the subject "they" of line 2 as its naming.

Example 8 (*Wall Street Journal*)

Workers dumped large burlap sacks of the imported material into a huge bin, poured in cotton and acetate fibers and mechanically mixed the dry fibers in a process used to make filters.

The naming-telling relationship in this text can be illustrated by NIS:

Workers dumped large burlap sacks of the imported material into a huge bin
poured in cotton and acetate fibers
and mechanically mixed the dry fibers in a process
‖ used to make filters .

Workers dumped large burlap sacks of the imported material into a huge bin in a process used to make filters.
Workers poured in cotton and acetate fibers in a process used to make filters
Workers and mechanically mixed the dry fibers in a process
‖ a process used to make filters .

Figure 10: The Influx Pattern in English.

Line 1 and line 2 need to share the same tail of telling in line 3 "in a process used to make filters", thus the NT clause can be constructed by Influx Pattern, which is to connect the tail of the line 3 to the end of line 1 and line 2. At the same time, the last two lines need a supplementary naming from line 1's subject.

In our English corpus, 99% of NT clauses can be constructed by these five patterns.

5 The nature of the NT clause in Chinese and English texts and the explanation from a cognitive perspective

The following statistics are from:

- Chinese corpus, 187 long texts with 30,963 NT clauses;
- English corpus, 93 short texts with 4,819 NT clauses.

Except for the types of NT clauses listed above, these NT clauses include a few subject ellipsis clause and incompletable clauses. Subject ellipsis clauses can be supplemented with a subject, while for an incompletable clause, it is impossible to supplement missing components.

5.1 Broad Coverage

Within this study, the Chinese and English texts can be covered by NT clauses, i.e. a text can be dissected into sequences of NT clauses, each word belongs to at least one NT clause, and a text is the combination of NT clauses. In the Chinese corpus, there are 2,044 incompletable clauses, 547 subject ellipsis clauses, with a total of 2,591 clauses, which accounts to 8.3% of the NT clauses; in the English corpus, there are 32 incompletable clauses, accounting to 0.66% of NT clauses, without any subject ellipsis clauses.

From a cognitive perspective, naming in an NT clause is a target of cognition, while telling is the content of cognition. Therefore, the NT clause is a basic cognition unit. The fact that NT clauses cover the whole text means that complex cognition forms are made up of basic cognition forms.

5.2 Order-preservation

The original texts in both the Chinese and the English corpus are one-dimensional structures. The NIS is an intermediate form of dissecting original texts into NT clauses, and has a two-dimensional structure. This process keeps the word sequence in the original text intact. To be more specific, for any two words, such as A and B, if A is to the left of B in the original text, then in the NIS, A is either to the left of B or above B, or vice versa.

Both the speech stream and text stream of natural language are linear. The words enter short-term memory of the human brain by their original order. Long-distance adjustment of word order is very hard because the capacity of the short-term memory is very limited. Order-preservation suits the limitations of brain cognition.

5.3 Non-transgressiveness

Naming is topic by and large, and one naming can be explained by several tellings. Under most circumstances, if one new naming-telling relationship occurs, replacing the old naming-telling relationship, then the component in the old naming-telling relationship cannot be shared as a naming by another telling following the new relationship. In another words, the component in the old naming-telling relationship cannot build another naming-telling relationship which trespasses on the new naming-telling relationship.

It is acceptable to say "他衣服笔挺，面料很讲究，鼻梁上架着一副金丝眼镜。" (His clothes are immaculate, and made of fine material, with a pair of gold-framed glasses resting on the ridge of his nose.), but not "他衣服笔挺，鼻梁上架着一副金丝眼镜，面料很讲究。" (His clothes are immaculate, with a pair of gold-framed glasses resting on the ridge of his nose, made of high fine material.） This is because the naming "衣服" (clothes) in the first line cannot trespass on the naming-telling relationship of the "鼻梁上" (on the ridge of his nose) as a naming. Therefore, the naming "衣服" (clothes) cannot be shared by the third P-clause in the second example.

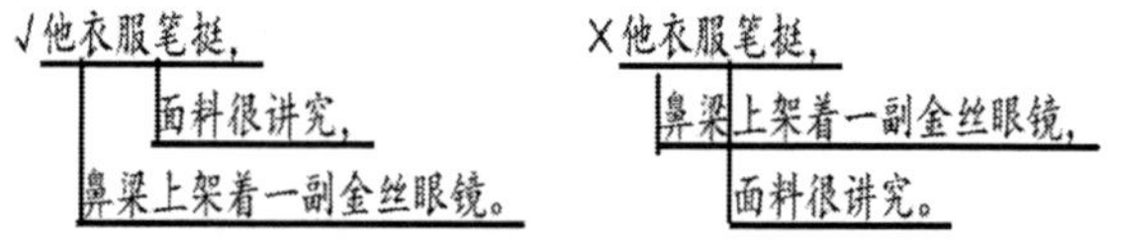

Figure 11: The non-transgressiveness of naming-telling relationship in Chinese.

Naming-telling relationship in English has the same property.

Example 9 (by the researcher)

It is acceptable to say "John has a son working in China, and Mary has a daughter studying in the USA.", but it is not acceptable to say "John has a son, and Mary has a daughter studying in the USA, working in China." This is because the naming "a son" cannot trespass the naming-telling relationship of the naming "Mary" and "daughter" to be shared by "working in China".

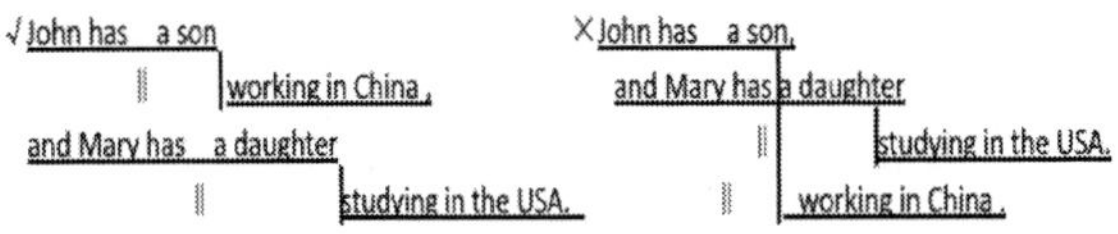

Figure 12: The non-transgressiveness of naming-telling relationship in English.

In our corpus of 30,963 Chinese NT clauses, there are 83 instances of trespassing, which accounts to 0.3%; 4,819 English NT clauses show only 4 instances of trespassing, accounting to 0.1%. 99% of both Chinese and English NT clauses do not trespass. For the few instances of trespassing NT clauses, they offer pragmatic background information. In example 10, the naming in line 1 and the telling in line 5 form a NT clause. This NT clause trespasses on the NT clause in line 4 which expresses the reason of the line 3.

Example 10 (*Wall Street Journal*)

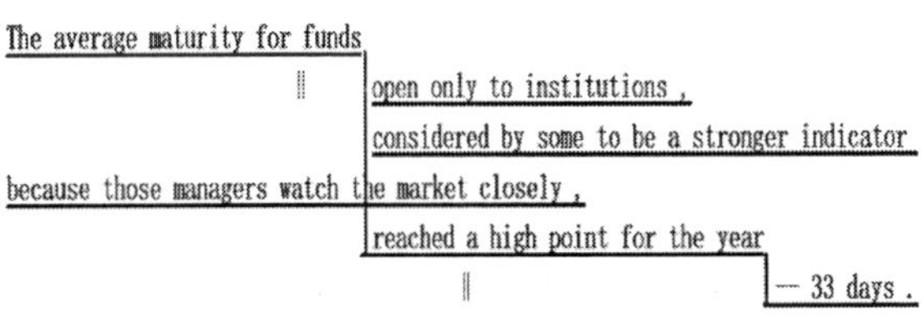

Figure 13: An example of trespassing on the naming-telling relationship.

The cognitive mechanism of the brain needs to process all tellings of a naming before going on to process the next naming and its tellings, so it is not likely for several tellings of different namings be processed all at the same time. The non-transgressiveness of the naming-telling relationship suits such constraint on cognition.

5.4 Syntactic well-formedness

Both in the Chinese or the English corpus, a part of NT clauses constitutes a grammatical SV structure, i.e., they are syntactically well-formed, and, while another part of the NT clauses is not syntactically well-formed.

In our corpus, 1,963 Chinese NT clauses (out of 30,963) are not syntactically well-formed, which makes up for 6.3%; while 2,463 English NT clauses (out of 4,819) are not syntactically well-formed, which accounts for 51.1%.

A part of the Chinese NT clauses is not syntactically well-formed, because when a naming is connected with its one telling sharing it and constructs an NT clause, the punctuation between them is discarded, causing some semantic relationship markers to be missing or redundant. Adding or deleting such markers can ensure the syntactical well-formedness. For instance, in this sentence "邯郸市在河北省南部，京广铁路穿城而过。" (Handan is in the south of Hebei province, Jing-Guang railway passes through the city), the second P-clause corresponds to the NT clause "邯郸市京广铁路穿城而过" (Handan Jing-Guang railway passes through the city). The semantic relationship between "邯郸市" (Handan) and "京广铁路" (Jing-Guang railway) is not clear, resulting in an awkward clause. We can add "有" (in…there is) to express existential meaning, thus forming the clause "邯郸市有京广铁路穿城而过" (In Handan, there is the Jing-Guang railway passing through the city), which is syntactically correct. Since Chinese grammatical rules are not as strict as English ones, Chinese NT clauses have a lower ratio of ungrammaticality.

In English, the syntactical well-formedness problem in NT clauses is also due to the connection of naming and telling which may result in the missing and redundancy of some connective component. For example, if the telling is a nonrestrictive verb phrase, it usually needs to add an auxiliary "be" to ensure syntacticality. Since English is more rule-governed than Chinese, English has far higher proportion of syntacticality problems.

Even though both Chinese and English NT clauses may exhibit problems in syntactical well-formedness, based on the above analysis, these problems can be solved by adding or deleting some connective component in a finite range. Therefore, all English and Chinese NT clause are syntactical by and large. By this analysis, in human cognition, an NT clause can be processed simply as a common clause, this attribute meeting the feasibility of NT clause cognition.

5.5 Distribution of NT clause construction patterns

In section 3 and 4, we listed five patterns of the NT clause for both Chinese and English. Among them, the Enclosed Chunk Pattern represents relation between two groups of NT clauses. Therefore, the NT clause can be classified into following six categories: the original SV structure, constructed with a Stack Pattern, Back Position Pattern, New Branch Pattern, or Influx Pattern, and others.

According to statistics in our corpus, the numbers and the proportions of the six categories in Chinese and English are following:

Pattern	Chinese		English	
	No.	Per.(%)	No.	Per.(%)
Original	11970	38.70	2420	50.20
Stack	16449	53.10	515	10.70
Back Position	162	0.50	145	3.00
New Branch	1056	3.40	1723	35.80
Influx	650	2.10	13	0.30
Other	676	2.20	3	0.10
NT clause total	30963	100	4819	100

Table 1: The distribution of NT clause constructing patterns in Chinese and English.

All the NT clauses in the category of "other" are instances of ellipsis which cannot be covered by our patterns. Among the 676 Chinese NT clauses, 547 are subjectless, and 129 are without middle parts; in English, three instances are have no middle parts. All these ellipses are related to specific patterns that are not discussed further in the present study.

For both Chinese and English, there are only a few instances of "other" categories. The Stack Pattern, Back Position Pattern, New Branch Pattern and Influx Pattern cover the majority of non-original SV structure NT clauses. Thus, the four patterns are essential for the NT clause. Section 3 of this study presents the NT clause construction mechanism of the Stack Pattern. This pattern can be assumed as one kind of human cognition mechanism. In Chinese, it is not uncommon that one naming goes with dozens of tellings. A naming can be connected with a telling which follows after dozens of P-clauses. This phenomenon is surprising, considering that the human brain has only 7±2 units of short term memory. However, if the human brain does follow the Stack Pattern to process, old tellings are discarded constantly, and the naming is always stored in our short term memory to form a connection with the telling, then this phenomenon is no longer strange. Therefore, the Stack Pattern is a reasonable explanation of cognitive brain function for the NT clause. Similarly, the Back Position Pattern, New Branch Pattern and Influx Pattern can be explained in ways which are not covered in detail in this study.

As shown in the above table, both the Back Position Pattern and Influx Pattern have a low frequency in either corpus. Considering this from a cognitive perspective, the Back Position Pattern cannot complete the cognition of the NT clause right after the occurrence of a telling; instead, the telling has to be stored temporarily to await its naming. At the same time, in the Influx Pattern, the front part of the telling occur first, and this part also has to be stored first to await its later part. These two processing patterns of NT clauses both pose high demands on time and space, and therefore their low frequency in the corpora is perhaps unavoidable.

As shown in the table, both the Chinese and English NT clause demonstrate different frequencies for these four patterns. The Chinese NT clause shows higher proportions for the Stack Pattern and the Influx Pattern than English, while the New Branch Pattern and the Back Position Pattern are lower than in English. This frequency difference is attributed to grammatical difference. Taking the Stack Pattern as an example, the Chinese expression usually moves from bigger concepts to smaller concepts, which is suitable to the progressively layered structure of the Stack Pattern. In contrast, the English expression moves from smaller concepts to bigger concepts, which is not suitable for the Stack Pattern. To take another example, for the New Branch Pattern, the English NT clause takes relative clause, preposition phrase or non-restrictive verbal phrase as its telling, and usually they have obvious markers causing less cognitive burden on the brain; however, Chinese does not have similar markers, so in most cases, it has to rely on semantic coordination to distinguish its meaning, and thus exhibits a heavier cognitive load.

6 Conclusion

This study puts forward the concepts of NT clause, dividing linear texts into a two-dimensional plane structure, and drawing up five patterns for constructing the NT clause. Through the annotation of corpus, this study discovered that both Chinese and English texts are formed through combinations of NT clauses according to these five patterns. The construction of the NT clause is order-preserving, non-transgressive, and syntactically well-formed. These features of the NT clause can be explained by appealing to cognitive mechanisms.

In the fields of linguistics and computational linguistics, the theories and methods of clause complex, topic and zero anaphora are related to our study. The kernel of our contribution is the discovery of formal patterns for constructing the NT clause. Based on these patterns, a syntactic platform suiting to both Chinese and English can be built. On the platform the MT of long sentences is decomposed to three steps: NT clause parsing in source language, translation of NT clauses, and assembling the NT clauses in target language. These steps are independent of each other. In this procedure, the first and third steps involve only one language and only the second step involves two languages. Moreover, the NT clauses handled in the second step have smaller scale and simpler structures than long sentence, so that they may be translated easier. This method, expected to ease the difficulties of long sentences in MT, will be discussed in another paper.

Acknowledgments

This research is sponsored by fund of Center for Translation Studies, Guangdong University of Foreign Studies (CTS2014-13) and supported by Innovative School Project in Higher Education of Guangdong, China (GWTP-LH-2015-10) and National Natural Science Foundation of China (61171129).

References

Carnie, Andrew. 2013. *Syntax: A Generative Introduction*, 3rd ed. Blackwell Publishing Ltd., West Sussex.

Dalrymple, Mary. 2001. *Lexical Functional Grammar*, volume 34 of Syntax and Semantics. Academic Press, New York.

Halliday, M.A.K. 1994. *Introduction to Functional Grammar*, 2nd ed. Edward Arnold, London.

Pollard, Carl & Ivan A. Sag. 1994. *Head-driven phrase structure grammar*. University of Chicago Press, Chicago.

Shen, Jiaxuan. 2013. Can predicates be nominals? *Foreign Studies*, 2013, 1(1): 1-13.

Song, Rou. 2013. Stream model of Generalized Topic Structure in Chinese text. *Studies of the Chinese Language*, 2013(6): 483-494.

Towards Semantic-based Hybrid Machine Translation between Bulgarian and English

Kiril Simov and **Petya Osenova** and **Alex Popov**
Linguistic Modelling Department, IICT-BAS
kivs|petya|alex.popov@bultreebank.org

Abstract

The paper focuses on the creation of a semantic-based hybrid Machine Translation system between Bulgarian and English in the domain of Information Technology. The preprocessing strategies are presented. A method for the substitution of English word forms with the synsets or Bulgarian representative lemmas is discussed. Finally, the creation of a factored model in the Moses system is described.

1 Introduction

In this paper we present first results from the implementation of a hybrid machine translation system between Bulgarian and English (en↔bg) using Word Sense Annotation (WSD) of the source language. There is an existing line of research that aims to combine the advantages of competing approaches to machine translation in a hybrid framework. (Thurmair, 2009) summarized several different architectures of hybrid systems using SMT and RBMT systems. Some widely explored ones are: 1) using an SMT to post-edit the outputs of an RBMT; 2) selecting the best translations from several hypotheses coming from different SMT/RBMT systems; and 3) selecting the best segments (phrases or words) from different hypotheses. In our case, after WSD, we use the alignment between Bulgarian and English WordNets for the generation of rules for word substitution. On the basis of these rules we generate a corpus with factors, on which the Moses system (Koehn et al., 2007) is trained: word forms, lemmas and POS tags as factors. Although we have not improved the baseline, the substitution rules have proven helpful. We plan to generate more sophisticated rules in our future work.

The structure of the paper is as follows: in the next section the related work is presented. Section 3 describes the workflow of the Parallel Corpora Processing. Section 4 outlines the experiments that have been conducted. Section 5 introduces some discussion on the results and concludes the paper.

2 Related Work

Previous work on using WSD for SMT has yielded mixed results. (Carpuat and Wu, 2005) report a negative impact on BLEU scores. They used a supervised WSD system to select translation candidates for the SMT system, but, contrary to common sense expectations, this only made the translation model perform worse. Several reasons for this are suggested, chiefly that the SMT model works well enough on its own and state-of-the-art WSD systems cannot really boost it in a significant number of cases, and also that SMT architectures might not be well-adapted to make use of the output of WSD systems. (Cabezas and Resnik, 2005) present an approach to using WSD for SMT, whereby target language lexical items are treated as "sense tags", given as soft translation alternatives to the translation model, which chooses the final version in accordance with its language model. The study reported a small gain against a base-

Proceedings of the 2nd Workshop on Semantics-Driven Machine Translation, pages 22–26,
San Diego, California, June 16, 2016.

line that is, according to the authors, stronger than the one used in (Carpuat and Wu, 2005). (Vickrey et al., 2005) recasts WSD as a translation task, defining the different sense options for the separate words as the words or phrases aligned to them in a parallel corpus. The authors demonstrate that this approach is successful, as tested on word translation and blank-filling, thus showing that WSD and SMT have a lot in common and improving one should be helpful for improving the other.

(Chan et al., 2007) present another study in which WSD is beneficial to SMT. Disambiguation is performed between the possible translations of each source phrase. Translations are selected so as to maximize the length of the chunk proposed by the WSD model; the score provided by the WSD model is also taken into consideration. This approach yields a statistically significant improvement in terms of BLEU score. In a study that builds on their previously discouraging results, (Carpuat and Wu, 2007) show how a deeper integration of WSD into SMT systems can help systematically and significantly. Instead of performing disambiguation on single words, their system performs multiword phrasal disambiguation, thus achieving improvements over the baseline, as measured by eight different translation metrics. The rich context provided by the supervised WSD system helps rank correct translations higher than erroneous ones suggested by the baseline SMT system; also, it helps the decoder pick longer translation sequences, which often results in better translations.

3 Parallel Corpora Processing

We are building a machine translation system between Bulgarian and English that can support the automatic identification of appropriate answers to user questions in a multilingual question/answering system. The domain of interest is related to information technology, smart phones and related devices and technologies. We have three domain-specific corpora of a thousand real-world question-answer pairs each - called Batch1, Batch2 and Batch3, respectively. In the experiments reported here, we exploit Batch1 for tuning the translation model and Batch3 for testing. For some experiments we have divided the questions from the answers. Then the two subcorpora have been denoted with "a" and "q" subscripts: Batch3a and Batch3q.

As training data we used the following corpora: the Setimes parallel corpus, the Europarl parallel corpus and a corpus created on the basis of the documentation of LibreOffice. The corpora are linguistically processed with the IXA[1] pipeline for the English part and the BTB pipeline for the Bulgarian. The analyses include POS tagging, lemmatization and WSD, using the UKB system[2], which provides graph-based methods for Word Sense Disambiguation and measuring lexical similarity. The tool uses the Personalized PageRank algorithm, described in Agirre and Soroa (2009). It has been used to perform Named Entity Disambiguation as well (Agirre et al., 2015). We have exploited the mapping between Bulgarian WordNet (BTB-WordNet) and Princeton English WordNet (PWN) in order to perform the Bulgarian WSD task — (Simov et al., 2015a).

For the baseline MT system, the following factors have been constructed: WordForm|Lemma|POStag. We have trained the Moses system using these factors. The results are presented in Table 1.

We also explored the impact of the bilingual morphological lexicons in the translation process, due to the occurrences of the so-called out-of-training word forms in the texts. See more in (Simov et al., 2015b). The bilingual lexicon was constructed by exploiting the following resources: BTB-Morphological lexicon containing all word-forms for more than 110 000 Bulgarian lemmas; BTB-bilingual Bulgarian-English lexicons (with about 8000 entries); English Wiktionary. From it the English word-forms were extracted for the English lemmas. Then we mapped the word-form lexicons for both languages to the corresponding part of the bilingual

[1]http://ixa2.si.ehu.es/ixa-pipes/

[2]http://ixa2.si.ehu.es/ukb/

lexicon. Afterwards, the corresponding word-forms were aligned on the basis of their morphological features like *number* (singular, plural); *degree* (comparative, superlative); *definiteness* (definite, indefinite), etc.

The lexicon represents more than 70 000 aligned word-forms. It was added to the training data. The results show the positive impact of the wordform-aligned parallel lexicon on the translation in both directions.

Our goal was to check the impact of WSD on this type of factor-based MT. The very first approach was to substitute the word form or lemma in the source text with a WordNet ID as a representation of the concept encoded by the corresponding synset. Additionally, we selected an appropriate lemma in the target language for the synset. Thus we relied on the concept information returned by the WSD software for the source text in two ways: a) to use the synset ID directly as a factor, or b) choose a *representative lemma* in the target language for that synset and present this representative lemma as a factor (in addition to the source word-form factor). The motivation for using representative lemmas in the target language is as follows: we aim at unifying the various synsets with similar translations in the target language. For example, in the en→bg direction, the two concepts referred by *donor*: `wn30-10025730-n` ("person who makes a gift of property") and `wn30-10026058-n` ("a medical term denoting someone who gives blood or tissue or an organ to be used in another person") are very close to each other, but they have the same translation in Bulgarian: *донор*. The representative word is selected on the basis of a frequency list of Bulgarian lemmas.

4 Experiments

Three experiments have been performed: using synset IDs returned by the WSD software (ExpA); using representative target language lemmas for the synsets returned by the WSD software (ExpB); using representative target lemmas where the WSD software is run on domain-adapted wordnets, extended with domain gazetteers and terms (ExpC). The experiments for en→bg were performed through these steps: (1) annotation of the English text with the IXA pipeline, including tokenization, sentence splitting, part-of-speech tagging and word sense annotation with UKB; (2) substitution of the English word form with the synset (in ExpA) or Bulgarian representative lemma (in ExpB and ExpC); and (3) creating a factored model in the Moses system. In the direction bg→en we performed similar processing. Additionally, we provided part-of-speech tags[3] (PoS) from the pipeline, as well as the source language lemma, as factors for Moses. The PoS factor is important for Bulgarian, since Bulgarian is a morphologically rich language. Here is an example for the procedure we performed with respect to the training, testing and tuning tasks:

English sentence:
This is real progress ...

English sentence with factors:
this|this|dt is|be|vbz реален|real|jj напредък|progress|nn .|.|.

Bulgarian sentence with factors:
това|това|pd е|съм|vx реален|реален|a напредък|напредък|nc .|.|pu

Bulgarian sentence:
Това е реален напредък.

In order to adapt the semantic processing, we incorporated a Linked Open Data resource (DB-Pedia) in the en↔bg experiments via a mapping of the DBpedia ontology to WordNet. Our goal was to use again the IXA pipeline for the WSD task, similarly to the lexical semantics experiments. Unfortunately, the DBpedia ontology contains very few relevant classes, like *software, website, database.* For that reason, we decided to use an additional ontology created in a previous European project, LT4eL,[4] which covers about 1500 classes in the domain of Information technology. This ontology is already aligned to OntoWordNet (Gangemi et al., 2003), which is the basis for the extension of the existing word-

[3]In our case PoS tags include some morphosyntactic features.

[4]http://www.lt4el.eu/

System	Source factors	Domain terms	en→bg BLEU	en→bg NIST	bg→en BLEU	bg→en NIST
baseline	form	no	17.72	–	22.56	–
ExpA	synset-id|form, lemma, PoS	no	16.23	4.81	16.72	4.99
ExpB	repres-lemma|form, lemma, PoS	no	17.23	4.95	20.05	5.61
ExpC	repres-lemma|form, lemma, PoS	yes	17.41	4.98	19.92	5.58

Table 1: BLEU and NIST results of en↔bg experiments with concepts on Batch3 (Batch3a for en→bg and Batch3q for bg→en). The baseline is Pilot 0, where no synsets are used. In ExpA, the synset ID is added (if it exists). In ExpB, *repres-lemma* is added, which is a representative target language lemma for the given (source language) synset. ExpC is the same as ExpB, but the WSD resource used was enriched with domain terms.

nets as used by the WSD system (UKB). Then we performed the substitution of synsets with selected representative target language lemmas and trained the Moses system with the following factors: SubstitutedWordform[5], Lemma, PoS tag.[6] Table 1 presents the results. All three en↔bg experiments with lexical semantics show a drop in the results with respect to the baseline. But the addition of substituted lemmas improves over the usage of the concept itself (synset-id). The addition of domain knowledge also increases the performance. This justifies further experiments in the direction of extending the rules for substitution of the source language chunks with target language chunks.

5 Discussion and Conclusions

Here we reported on the initial steps of implementation of hybrid semantic statistical MT systems between Bulgarian and English. Our next development goal is to improve on the initial translation steps from the source to the target language by learning transfer rules from corpora. The main points of improvement will be:

Selection of appropriate representative lemma for a given sense. The current mechanism for selection of a representative lemma for a given WordNet synset is not the most appropriate. Thus we envisage the following options. First, word embeddings are trained on large corpora (which are first lemmatized). Then, for the lemmas in the synset we select their vectors and calculate their centroid. Our hope is that the centroid will be the best vector representation of the synset in the vector space. Afterwards, as a representative lemma we will select the lemma with a vector that is closest to the centroid. If more than one lemmas are very close to the centroid, we will look for additional information like frequency counts in the corpus, or we will perform manual selection.

Processing of analytical verb forms. Both languages in the translation pair have rich analytical verb complexes. On the basis of aligned parallel corpora, we will collect information about the most frequent translations. Then, with the help of the statistics we will construct rules for the translation of verbs between languages. These rules will be integrated with the rules for selection of the representative lemmas for verbal synsets.

Transfer of relations including close-class words. By using sense-annotated parallel corpora, we plan to learn the most frequent translations of prepositions between words that belong to given senses in both wordnets.

Using such rules we expect to be able to translate bigger portions of the source language text to the target language, and in this way to improve the overall translation.

Acknowledgments

This research has received partial funding from the EC's FP7 under grant agreement number 610516: "QTLeap: Quality Translation by Deep Language Engineering Approaches".

[5]For some word forms like prepositions, conjunctions, etc., the original word-form is kept.

[6]The parameters for training the Moses system are: `--translation-factors 0,2-0,2+1,2-0,2 --decoding-steps t0:t1`

References

Eneko Agirre and Aitor Soroa. 2009. Personalizing PageRank for word sense disambiguation. In *Proceedings of the 12th Conference of the European Chapter of the ACL (EACL 2009)*, pages 33–41, Athens, Greece, March. Association for Computational Linguistics.

Eneko Agirre, Ander Barrena, and Aitor Soroa. 2015. Studying the wikipedia hyperlink graph for relatedness and disambiguation. *arXiv preprint arXiv:1503.01655*.

Clara Cabezas and Philip Resnik. 2005. Using wsd techniques for lexical selection in statistical machine. Technical report, Translation Technical report CS-TR-4736.

Marine Carpuat and Dekai Wu. 2005. Word sense disambiguation vs. statistical machine translation. In *Proceedings of the 43rd Annual Meeting on Association for Computational Linguistics*, pages 387–394. Association for Computational Linguistics.

Marine Carpuat and Dekai Wu. 2007. Improving statistical machine translation using word sense disambiguation. In *EMNLP-CoNLL*, volume 7, pages 61–72.

Yee Seng Chan, Hwee Tou Ng, and David Chiang. 2007. Word sense disambiguation improves statistical machine translation. In *Annual Meeting-Association for Computational Linguistics*, volume 45, page 33. Citeseer.

Aldo Gangemi, Roberto Navigli, and Paola Velardi. 2003. The ontowordnet project: Extension and axiomatization of conceptual relations in wordnet. In Robert Meersman, Zahir Tari, and DouglasC. Schmidt, editors, *On The Move to Meaningful Internet Systems 2003: CoopIS, DOA, and ODBASE*, volume 2888 of *Lecture Notes in Computer Science*, pages 820–838. Springer Berlin Heidelberg.

Philipp Koehn, Hieu Hoang, Alexandra Birch, Chris Callison-Burch, Marcello Federico, Nicola Bertoldi, Brooke Cowan, Wade Shen, Christine Moran, Richard Zens, et al. 2007. Moses: Open Source Toolkit for Statistical Machine Translation. In *Proceedings of the 45th Annual Meeting of the ACL on Interactive Poster and Demonstration Sessions*, pages 177–180. Association for Computational Linguistics.

Kiril Simov, Alexander Popov, and Petya Osenova. 2015a. Improving word sense disambiguation with linguistic knowledge from a sense annotated treebank. In *Proceedings of the International Conference Recent Advances in Natural Language Processing*, pages 596–603.

Kiril Simov, Iliana Simova, Velislava Todorova, and Petya Osenova. 2015b. Factored Models for Deep Machine Translation. In *Proceedings of the 1st Deep Machine Translation Workshop (DMTW 2015)*, pages 97–105.

Gregor Thurmair. 2009. Comparing different architectures of hybrid machine translation systems. In *Proceedings of MT Summit XII.*

David Vickrey, Luke Biewald, Marc Teyssier, and Daphne Koller. 2005. Word-sense disambiguation for machine translation. In *Proceedings of the conference on Human Language Technology and Empirical Methods in Natural Language Processing*, pages 771–778. Association for Computational Linguistics.

Association for Computational Linguistics
209 N. Eighth Street
Stroudsburg, Pennsylvania 18360

ISBN 978-1-5108-2524-6

CURRAN ASSOCIATES INC.
proceedings.com